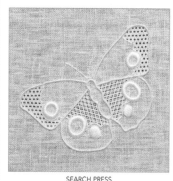

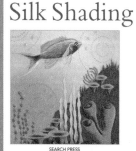

APPLIQUÉ

DEDICATION

This dedication is split two ways:
to my husband Rich for his humour and
support, and for everything he has been
unfortunate enough to learn about embroidery
– rather than his preference for cars and sport.
And to my parents, for their enthusiasm and
for backing what might be considered an
'unusual career choice'.

ACKNOWLEDGEMENTS

With special thanks to
Clare Rose. Thanks also go to
the Royal School of Needlework,
The Embroiderers' Guild, Chertsey Museum,
The Sunbury Millennium Embroidery Gallery,
Hastings Borough Council,
The D-Day Museum and to all those
inspirational students I teach.

First published in 2016

Search Press Limited
Wellwood, North Farm Road,
Tunbridge Wells, Kent TN2 3DR

Text and illustrations copyright
© Kate Cross 2016

Photographs by Paul Bricknell: 1, 2–3, 4–5,
8–9t, 13b, 15, 16, 17, 18, 19, 20, 21, 22, 23,
24, 25, 26, 27, 28, 29, 31, 34, 35, 36, 38, 39,
40, 42, 43, 44, 45, 46, 47, 48, 49, 50, 51, 52,
53 (steps 1–4), 54, 55, 56, 57, 58, 59, 60, 61,
62, 63, 64, 65, 66, 67, 68, 69, 70, 71, 72, 73,
78, 79, 86, 87, 88, 89, 90, 91, 92, 93, 95, 100,
101, 102, 108, 109, 110, 111, 112, 113, 114,
115, 116, 117, 118, 119, 120, 121, 122, 123,
124, 125

Photographs by Kate Cross: 14, 30, 32–33,
37, 75, 76, 77, 94, 98, 99

Other photographs:
7, all © The Royal School of Needlework
8b © Sunbury Millennium Embroidery
   Gallery
9b © Jane Francis
10, all © The Embroiderers' Guild
11t © Hastings Museum and Art Gallery
11b © Clare Rose
12 © D-Day Museum
13tc, tr © Chertsey Museum
41 © Auburn Claire Lucas

53bl, br © Fiona Hart
80 © The Embroiderers' Guild
81 © Linda Kilgore
82t © Michael Bingham
82b © Anne Rowan
83 © Mimi Chan
84 © Yukari Suai
85 © Fiona Hart
103 © Elaine Dunn
104t © Helen Robinson
104b © Teresa McAuliffe
105t © Annalee Levin
105b © Sara-Jane Dennis
106 © Alana Chenevix-Trench
107 © The Embroiderers' Guild

Design copyright © Search Press Ltd 2016

All rights reserved. No part of this book, text,
photographs or illustrations may be reproduced
or transmitted in any form or by any means
by print, photoprint, microfilm, microfiche,
photocopier, internet or in any way known
or as yet unknown, or stored in a retrieval
system, without written permission obtained
beforehand from Search Press.

ISBN: 978-1-78221-188-4

The Publishers and author can accept no
responsibility for any consequences arising
from the information, advice or instructions
given in this publication.

Readers are permitted to reproduce any
of the items/patterns in this book for their
personal use, or for the purposes of selling for
charity, free of charge and without the prior
permission of the Publishers. Any use of the
items/patterns for commercial purposes is
not permitted without the prior permission
of the Publishers.

Suppliers
For details of suppliers, please see page 127
and visit the Search Press website:
www.searchpress.com

For further information about the author's
work, please see:
www.bespokeembroidery.net

For more information about the RSN, its
courses, studio, shop and exhibitions, see
www.royal-needlework.org.uk

For information about the RSN degree
programme, see www.rsndegree.uk

Printed in China

KATE CROSS

APPLIQUÉ
TECHNIQUES, PROJECTS & PURE INSPIRATION

SEARCH PRESS

CONTENTS

RSN ROYAL SCHOOL OF NEEDLEWORK

THE ROYAL SCHOOL OF NEEDLEWORK

Founded in 1872, the Royal School of Needlework (RSN) is the international centre of excellence for the art of hand embroidery. It is based at Hampton Court Palace in west London but also offers courses across the UK, in the USA and Japan. Today it is a thriving, dynamic centre of teaching and learning, and believes that hand embroidery is a vital art form that impacts on many aspects of our lives from clothes to ceremonial outfits, and from home furnishings to textile art.

To enable and encourage people to learn the skill of hand embroidery the RSN offers courses from beginner to degree level. The wide range of short courses includes introductions to each of the stitch techniques the RSN uses, beginning with Introduction to Embroidery. The RSN's Certificate and Diploma in Technical Hand Embroidery offers students the opportunity to learn a range of techniques to a very high technical standard. The Future Tutors course is specifically designed for those pursuing a career in teaching technical hand embroidery. The RSN's BA (Hons) Degree course is the only UK degree course solely focussed on hand embroidery and offers students opportunities to learn core stitch techniques, which they are then encouraged to apply in contemporary and conceptual directions. Graduates can go on to find careers in embroidery relating to fashion, couture and costume; to interiors and soft furnishings or in the area of textile art including jewellery and millinery.

At its Hampton Court headquarters, the RSN welcomes people for all kind of events from private lessons to bespoke stitching holidays, intensive Certificate and Diploma studies, tours around our exhibitions, which comprise either pieces from our own textile collections or students' work, or study days looking at particular pieces or techniques from our Collection. Work by students and from the Collection also forms the core of a series of lectures and presentations available to those who cannot get to the RSN.

The RSN Collection of textiles comprises more than 2,000 pieces, all of which have been donated, because as a charity the RSN cannot afford to purchase additions. The pieces were given so that they would have a home for the future and to be used as a resource for students and researchers. The Collection comes from all over the world, illustrating many different techniques and approaches to stitch and embellishment.

The RSN Studio undertakes new commissions and conservation work for many different clients, including public institutions, places of worship, stately homes and private individuals, again illustrating the wide variety of roles embroidery can play, from altar frontals and vestments for churches to curtains, hangings and chair covers for homes and embroidered pictures as works of art.

Over the last few years the RSN has worked with a number of prestigious names including Sarah Burton OBE for Alexander McQueen, Vivienne Westwood's Studio for Red Carpet Green Dress, Patrick Grant's E Tautz, the late L'Wren Scott, Nicholas Oakwell Couture for the GREAT Britain Exhibition, the Jane Austen House Museum, Liberty London, the V&A Museum of Childhood and M&S and Oxfam for Shwopping.

For more information about the RSN, its courses, studio, shop and exhibitions, see www.royal-needlework.org.uk, and for its degree programme see www.rsndegree.uk.

Hampton Court Palace, Surrey, home of
the Royal School of Needlework

INTRODUCTION TO APPLIQUÉ

The term 'appliqué' literally means to 'put on' or 'apply' and derives from the French, *appliquer*. Within this book I am going to explore the various ways of applying fabrics on top of each other, giving you clear instruction and lots of inspiration. Appliqué can produce sensational and striking effects when carefully designed and worked with a range of fabrics, dyeing techniques, padding, threads and embroidery. It allows you to combine texture and colour and build up dimensions on fabric, both on the front and the reverse, at a relatively fast rate, which is why I like it so much. It is also an accessible technique – most embroiderers will already have a stash of fabrics somewhere in their home. Now is your chance to use up all those cherished but unused scrap fabrics!

Within my own working practice I relish the design process and I enjoy the freedom of combining appliqué with other embroidery techniques, which I have detailed later on in this book. Appliqué elements are mostly medium to large in scale and are usually designed for impact. Working small fabric pieces can sometimes inhibit the success of appliqué – it can be very easy to fray fiddly-sized pieces of material. To assist you as you learn, I have shared helpful tips and hints throughout this book and deliberately worked on a range of

The Village Panel
3 x 1m (9¾ x 3¼ft)

The Sunbury Millennium Embroidery was designed by John Stamp, based on an idea by David Brown, to celebrate the riverside village of Sunbury-on-Thames in the year 2000. Creating the Embroidery involved over 150 local embroiderers with varying skill levels and ages, mainly in the local community. The work was overseen by skilled local embroiderer Pamela Judd. The finished piece is a result of over 100,000 hours of dedicated effort.

shapes – some simple and some more complex – to help you make informed decisions about which appliqué techniques would work best for individual elements in your particular design.

The focus in this book will be the hand embroidery techniques I learned whilst completing my Royal School of Needlework apprenticeship, along with skills that I have continued to acquire since graduating. However, it is important to note that appliqué can be created using some sewing machine techniques too, so both hand and machine appliqué have been combined in some of the projects. I have shared my embroidery skills in a systematic and practical order, as I would do when teaching, so that you will build on your knowledge as you work through the book. My aim is to give you confidence with the techniques and inspire you to put them into practice using the correct methodology, while expressing your own creativity.

There is a range of beautiful work within this book that is both contemporary and historical, from a range of textile artists, which I hope will inspire you to generate your own ideas for design. I suggest you keep a notepad and pen to hand while reading as I'm certain you will start formulating ideas as you learn.

Smocked three-dimensional cupcakes
Each approximately 8cm (3¼in) tall and 6cm (2⅓in) wide
Kate Cross

These mouthwatering cupcakes were made using many different smocking techniques; I created wadded three-dimensional forms for the cake bases and then used lots of slip stitch to apply the cases and icing invisibly.

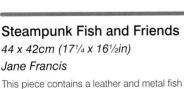

Steampunk Fish and Friends
44 x 42cm (17¼ x 16½in)
Jane Francis

This piece contains a leather and metal fish submarine with a metal and glass eyeball periscope. It is set against hand-dyed linen and features stumpwork coral and a leather octopus edged with gold. The island and seabed contain machine-embroidered seaweed, beads and hand-embroidered limpets and starfish.

HISTORY OF APPLIQUÉ

Appliqué has been in existence for thousands of years, both as an art form and as a way of preserving and embellishing garments. Appliqué is quite separate in technique from patchwork, where pieces are sewn together side by side; appliqué is worked as built-up layers of fabric. Different styles of and uses for appliqué have evolved and developed throughout history all around the world, and I will look at a few examples of this within the next few pages, with a particular focus on western Europe.

Given how widespread it has been, there is relatively little that remains of most of the appliqué created throughout history, as it was usually made to form part of everyday usable objects. One of the earliest known examples of appliqué is that of Tutankhamun's funeral wardrobe: decorative bands of embroidery were applied at each side of his sleeved tunic. But the extent of historical appliqué is greater than just clothing: appliqué has been found on an Egyptian funeral tent that dates back almost 3,000 years, while Ottoman tents, created from around the 16th century onwards, were adorned with appliqué in a huge array of materials such as linen, cotton, leather, velvet and satin. These pieces were worked to emulate woven patterns and were designed to display skill, prestige and wealth. Floor covers in the tents were created in the same way and combined with each other for incredible effect. Once the floor covers became worn, they were cut up and used for smaller items such as hangings and curtains.

But even further back than this – around 1,000 AD – embroidery was highly developed in Europe. English embroidery was particularly sought after and was traded throughout Europe and the Byzantine Empire up until the 14th century. This embroidery was known as *Opus Anglicanum* and combined highly prized lavish gold and silk embroidery. Appliqué was known as *Opus Conscutum* in Latin. In the West, appliqué found its niche in the church and court before it became widely practised in the home. Painted figures were applied to churchwork as slips and along with this, further slips of expensive silver gilt embroidery were applied, with the motifs edged with silver threads. Before mass production and easy trade routes brought down the cost, fabrics were extremely expensive; unusual textures and colours would have been hard to acquire, so incorporating these fabrics using appliqué was a way of displaying wealth and status.

Mola appliqués
Each 12 x 12cm (4¾ x 4¾in)

These are small samples of reverse appliqué worked by artist, tutor and collector Herta Puls, a leading expert in molas. They form part of one of her collections and were given to the Embroiderers' Guild after her death.

Methods of appliqué continued to develop during the 15th century, and during times of military unrest appliqué was considered to be time efficient compared with other embroidery techniques. Banners and flags often combined embroidery with appliqué for bold effect, right up until screen printing was developed in 1907. In Europe, the development of basic printing techniques in the 16th century led to both fashion and furnishings being embroidered for utilitarian use. The use of appliqué remained popular in ecclesiastical furnishings, especially in Spain and Italy, until the early 17th century, when Renaissance scrollwork and bold patterns echoed woven silks.

During the 17th century, the textile designs in Europe were increasingly influenced by trade objects and a fascination with the East. Appliqué was fashionable in the 17th century and this was partly because it could be used in combination with highly valued Indian chintzes. Indian chintz was printed in brilliant colours due to the advanced dyeing techniques that had been developed in India. In 17th-century Europe, an appliqué technique called Broderie Perse became very popular. Motifs were cut out from chintz fabric and applied to a fabric ground. Fabric edges were invisibly stitched down with buttonhole stitch, satin stitch or long and short stitch in order to stretch the expensive imported chintz as far as possible. The East India Company imported chintz into the UK, but it was banned from import in 1701, as it was felt that its popularity was a threat to the British textile industry. During the second half of the 18th century, chintz was produced in the UK, but this in turn initiated a decline in the Broderie Perse technique.

Drake and the Golden Hinde
274.5 x 91.5cm (108 x 36in)
Photograph courtesy of Hastings Museum & Art Gallery
Made by the Royal School of Needlework, this piece shows Queen Elizabeth I knighting Sir Francis Drake at Deptford in 1581.

Broderie Perse quilt centre
Centre: 60 x 60cm (23½ x 23½in);
quilt overall 195 x 195cm (76¾ x 76¾in)
Clare Rose

This centre panel in Broderie Perse is from a patchwork quilt, made using fabrics reproduced from an 1830s quilt in the Smithsonian Institution (Washington, DC, USA). It is made from cotton, hand-stitched and hand-quilted, and was created between 1995 and 2005.

The Overlord Embroidery, Panel 28: Distinguished Visitors go Ashore

90 x 240cm (35½ x 94½in)

Photograph courtesy of the D-Day Museum, Portsmouth

Designed by Sandra Lawrence and made by the Royal School of Needlework. Like many of the Overlord Embroidery panels, Panel 28 sums up several different aspects of the story of the Normandy Landings that began on D-Day, 6th June 1944. The foreground image shows Allied leaders making a visit to the Normandy beaches after D-Day. Left to right, they are: King George VI, General Dwight Eisenhower, General Sir Bernard Montgomery, Field Marshal Alan Brooke and Winston Churchill. The two sailors on the right represent PLUTO (Pipeline Under the Ocean), which was laid across the English Channel to pump fuel across to the Allied armies. In the sea behind them are sections of the Mulberry Harbours – artificial harbours built in sections by the Allies and towed across to Normandy where they were assembled.

By the 18th century, the craze for patchwork and appliqué had come back into fashion and was in full swing – this was epitomised by the production of new printed fabrics that were designed to be cut up to satisfy the demand. As fewer women were making their own clothes, soft furnishings and quilts were created to respond to fashions. Coverlets, or ornamental covers for beds, were also made in wealthy homes. Coverlets were a portable piece of work and often highly decorative, combining many techniques for show of skill and wealth of leisure time. It was in the United States that appliqué found its renaissance, as printed textiles from Europe or India were highly valued. Appliqué lends itself to more complex and curved shapes than the geometric shapes of patchwork pieces. Scraps would be saved and turned into quilts for warmth, or even clothes. These works became prized possessions, and today there are several collections of these works in many of the best US museums.

In the 19th century, a new craze for paper-cutting techniques evolved along with a technique known as Turkey Red Hawaiian appliqué, where emblems were cut from fabric and applied on a contrasting ground and sewn either by machine or with hand-finished edges. Advances in the production of calico (known as muslin in the US) and the British development of the copper plate printing method undermined the Indian chintz trade and by the end of the 19th century the British were producing cottons that rivalled the high-quality Indian goods.

By the 1860s, machines were producing lace and embroidery – this led to massive economic and social change, and a decline in hand embroidery. But since the Arts and Crafts movement in the 1880s there has been a desire to preserve traditional appliqué skills. In the first half of the 20th century, haute couture garments had embroidered slips and fabrics applied onto ground fabric in a show of wealth – a wonderful example of this is the

Lanvin dress, shown right, made in 1938, which features gold kid leather and sequins. The call for free expression in the 20th and 21st centuries and a focus on skill-based techniques has led to a resurgence in appliqué.

Dating back over the last few centuries, one of my favourite appliqué forms is called mola appliqué, which is from the San Blas Islands off the northern coast of Panama – an example of which can be seen below. Mola appliqué is a complex form of reverse appliqué, used to create colourful decorative panels that are used for women's blouses. Around seven layers of fabric are stitched together and designs and different coloured materials are revealed with each cut. The imagery is drawn from the Kuna people's history and culture – often incorporating animals or spiritual symbols. The colourful, bold shapes of this distinctive method of appliqué demonstrate just how versatile appliqué is.

Lanvin dress
The Chertsey Museum, Surrey

Evening dress of bias-cut red wool, appliquéd with gold kid leather and sequins, Jeanne Lanvin, 1938. From the Olive Matthews collection.

San Blas Mola
20 x 33cm (8 x 13in)
Unknown

This is a piece from my personal collection. It is a form of complex reverse appliqué worked with several layers of fabric and would have formed the front of a woman's or girl's blouse.

FABRICS

BACKGROUND FABRICS

Traditionally, appliqué is worked on a background of either calico (muslin) or linen, according to the fabrics that are being applied. Calico (muslin) is an inexpensive part-processed cotton that comes in three weights: light, medium and heavy. The medium-weight is generally the right density of weave for appliqué projects and has very little stretch, so acts as a very good support base. Calico (muslin) is used to give substance and support to appliqué work and reduce costs of using large quantities of expensive fabric backgrounds. It is readily available in most haberdashers. A good alternative, linen is used more often for banners and flags as it is robust and forms a thicker base. If your design calls for lots of layers of padding and fabric it may be best to use a calico (muslin) base, as it will be less bulky to stitch through than linen.

In some cases the backing fabric of your design may be sturdy enough to support your appliqué work without a base of calico (muslin) or linen. Thick fabrics such as upholstery-weight silk will not need an additional layer for support.

APPLIQUÉ FABRICS

For the projects in this book I have used a wide range of fabrics to demonstrate the effects that can be created. From leather and silk to tulle, linen and cotton, nothing is off limits, provided that you tension your work correctly. Experiment with fabric weights, patterns and colours to create wonderful contemporary effects. If you are new to appliqué and creating a design for the first time, I would advise that you use one type of fabric throughout your whole design. It is easiest to work with a set of fabrics that has the same tension and a similar movement. If you combine lots of different fabrics they may pucker and not sit well together – in time you will learn to tension your embroidery frame to accommodate this. My first choice of fabric would be cottons. Silks are also a good option, but they fray a little more readily than cottons.

When selecting fabrics for your design it is wise to use those that don't fray too much. I would advise against velvets or cords, or any other fabrics that have a high pile, especially if this is your first piece of appliqué (see tip box, right, for a tip on how to stabilise these fabrics). Synthetic fabrics with a plastic-like finish can slip and move when you apply them so, again, avoid these initially.

DYEING

Dyeing fabrics gives you the option to create bespoke effects and colours for your projects. I often use silk dyes, which are handy to use and work best if the fabric you are using is taut and crease-free. Silk dyes can be watered down and mixed to create the right colours. They can also be layered up if each layer is left to dry. If you want a soft background where dyes bleed into each other, apply a wash of water so that the dyes mix. Most silk dyes can also be used for cottons and linens, and they set with an iron on a high heat. Check the manufacturer's instructions prior to use.

Other dyes to try include acid dyes, procion dyes or natural dyes. You might also consider printing a design using a screen or a block, or using watercolour pencils for fine detail – but just remember that watercolours are not fixed as a dye would be.

Creating dye effects

Always dye or paint your fabric before applying it to the background calico (muslin). Don't try to do this once you have completed the framing-up process, as fabrics dry at different rates so it is inevitable that you will not get a smooth painted effect.

You can create some fantastic effects with paint and fabric. The sample below was created by painting silk dyes onto Habotai silk on a tight frame. To create interesting marks for texture, rock salt was scattered onto the dyed areas before they dried. Machining and fabrics were added once the dyes had dried.

Using iron-on interfacing to prevent fraying

Adding an iron-on interfacing, such as Vilene, stabilises fabrics, prevents stretch and fraying and retains a cut shape. It is very useful for fabrics such as velvet and cord or any other fabrics with a heavy pile. The interfacings can be purchased in a range of weights for use with different materials. When applying, sandwich the fabric in a folded sheet of baking paper to prevent any adhesive sticking to the iron.

Creating height
Pieces of carpet felt can be teased apart to create different heights where necessary.

PADDING

A crucial element of appliqué work is creating areas of relief and raised interest. There are many ways of doing this and padding is one of the most common. Traditionally, wool felt is used to create dimensions, and it can be layered up to create the desired height. You will apply the felt in layers, starting with a small piece, cut smaller than your design area, gradually layering up larger and larger pieces until you fill the design shape. See page 42 for further information. The felt gives a smooth finish to a raised area, making it easy to then apply another fabric on top.

Traditionally, carpet felt is used for building up high layers of relief in embroidery. However, if you cannot source carpet felt, a good alternative is extra thick 100 per cent wool felt. Both carpet felt and extra thick felt can be used to build up high reliefs over large areas. It is worth knowing that five layers of regular felt is equivalent to one layer of carpet felt, so for any area where you wish to achieve relief higher than five pieces of felt, use carpet felt layers instead.

To create a softer padded effect, toy stuffing and pulled apart wadding (batting) can be used to stuff flat applied appliqué pieces from the reverse of the fabric as a trapunto quilting technique, see page 47.

TOOLS

Any appliqué piece you work on should be carefully planned before you start stitching. Making sure that you have the fundamental tools to begin with is essential, and will make the project much more enjoyable to work on.

FRAMES

Appliqué looks most beautiful when fabrics are smoothly applied without any puckering – unless the puckering is a deliberate effect – so I would strongly advise that you work in a frame rather than simply working with the fabric in your hand. Without a frame, tensioning the fabrics evenly is incredibly difficult. The size of your embroidery will determine what frame you use.

SLATE FRAMES

I usually work on a slate frame (see top right, and pages 24–29 for information about framing up), as the large surface area gives me the most scope for design. A slate frame is made up of four lengths of wood. There are two 'rollers', which sit at the top and bottom of the frame. These have a strip of webbing attached, to which you will sew your fabric. The other two supports, which sit on the left and right, are full of holes and are called the 'arms'. A slate frame is used in conjunction with a trestle so that you can sit at your frame. Slate frames create a tight even tension and are very useful for working large projects.

RING FRAMES

If your design is relatively small, you may find that a ring frame is more appropriate than a slate frame, as it will be easier to transport and less expensive (see bottom left, and pages 22–23 for information on framing up).

Ring frames come in many shapes and sizes, some of which are hand-held while others clamp to tables or are inserted with a dowel to a seat base so that the embroiderer can stitch with both hands. Table frames and seat frames are my preferred options, as you can stitch much faster with two hands free.

Appliqué designs often call for areas of intense embroidery that are then applied over padding for relief – these are known as slips. Ring frames are very useful for working on slips as they allow you to create many different slips in advance and have them ready for applying onto a main frame.

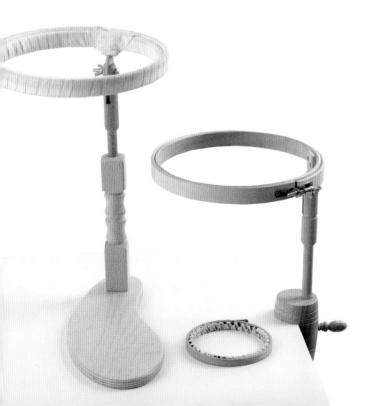

Getting the best from a ring frame

Tighten the ring frame every time you work, to ensure that you keep the same tight tension on the fabric. Remove the ring frame when not in use, to try to prevent ring marks forming on the fabric. Binding a frame with bias binding or a cotton fabric such as calico (muslin) will ensure you get a tight tension to your framed fabric.

NEEDLES

I work with a small embroidery needle when applying fabrics as it allows me to be very precise with my stitches. I use a larger chenille needle for plunging any threads to the reverse of the frame and a curved needle for casting off the ends of cords or couched threads. I also use a bracing needle for framing up. Generally the higher the number of the needle the smaller the needle is. See pages 126–127 for a full guide to different needle types.

PINS

There is an enormous variety of pins available, including specialist types for silks, and two-pronged types for an extra secure grip. I like glass-headed pins as they are easy to grip.

IRON

I use a mini-iron with attachments that allows me to handle small, fiddly pieces of fabric. A normal iron can be used when handling larger pieces.

SCISSORS

Scissors are important for appliqué and you can buy many different types. I use a curved pair for cutting off fabrics and threads on the front of the frame as it avoids any nicks in the fabric. Appliqué scissors are useful for reverse appliqué as they have a little metal bobble on the underside of the lower blade, which prevents unwanted cutting through lower layers of fabric. Fabric shears are also useful when cutting large pieces of fabric.

TAPE MEASURE

Your tape measure is used for measuring up fabrics, finding the mid-point of your fabric when framing up and for ensuring measurements done by eye for placement of appliqué pieces are true.

BEESWAX

This is traditionally used for strengthening machine threads when a tight pull is required. It is also used when working with metal threads to prevent the thread fraying or breaking and to create lubrication.

THIMBLE

Thimbles help to protect fingers and are useful when sewing and pushing a needle up through a large amount of padding, or when working on tough jobs. If a metal thimble is uncomfortable, leather and plastic types are also available.

STRING

This is used for framing up your slate frame (see pages 24–29).

NEEDLE GRABBER

This piece of rubber is very useful for pulling needles through padding. It has a rough texture which, when used with a needle, grips and can help to pull through fabric. This is a very useful item if you don't get on with thimbles.

SOFT BRUSH

I use a baby brush to brush off excess pounce once a design is painted and has dried on the fabric.

MARKING TOOLS

PENS

There is a wide range of pens on the market. Transfer pens are designed to be used with fabrics with some man-made content, for example poly-cottons. They are not suitable for fine design as the lines tend to grow in translation. Permanent markers are designed to be stable and fast on most materials. Friction pens can be drawn onto fabric and then removed by rubbing using the 'friction ball' on the end of the pen, or with an iron. But these marks can reappear if exposed to extreme temperatures, so be cautious where you use them in your work. My preference is for an HB lead propelling pencil.

PAINT

When using paint to mark designs on fabric I would advise using a watercolour. Alternatively, if the textile is likely to get wet, an oil paint would be preferable. Do not use a paint that is plastic-based.

WATERCOLOUR PENCILS

These are a good substitute when you don't want to use watercolour paint, or you are using a dark fabric where an HB pencil will not show up.

POUNCE

Pounce is traditionally white or black. Black pounce is made from ground up charcoal and white pounce is made from ground cuttlefish. White pounce is for use on darker fabrics and the black for use on lighter fabrics. Alternatively, to make a mid-colour, grey can be made by mixing the black and the white together once ground. Apply with a pounce pad – a rolled piece of fabric (see left).

PRICKING TOOL

You will need to use a pricking tool, or needle, to pierce a tracing paper base to push the pounce through (see page 34).

TAILORS' CHALK

Chalk is available in different colours in the form of propelling pens, which are easy to draw with. Be aware that after a couple of hours of work the line will fade and will need to be re-drawn.

Trying out your pens

It is always worth double checking that the pen does what it says on the packaging. Do a test on a scrap piece of fabric. Draw onto the fabric, let the pen dry and then blot some water onto the pen line and then dab this with tissue to see if the pen line stays or lifts off. If you have any doubts, use a lead pencil or paint using the 'prick and pounce' method (see pages 34–35).

THREADS

You will need machine threads – polyester or cotton – for applying felts and fabrics. There is a vast range of threads on the market – I have a range of silks, stranded cottons, linen threads and wool, which I will choose from according to the design I am working on. The threads can be matt, shiny, metallic, fine or chunky – ultimately the selection is a design decision. Shop around and pick up textures and colours that appeal to you.

For most appliqué edges, stranded cottons are the best choice, and I also use these when making cords. Metal threads can be purchased from specialist suppliers and there is a wide range of differing textures and colours available. They can be used in designs to cover applied edges as they can be couched over using Japanese thread, metal cords, passing thread and pearl-purl. Sometimes they are cut to form purls and a thread is passed through the middle – rather like using a bead. Wires can also be used to create dimension (see the Poppy project, pages 94–102).

HABERDASHERY

RIBBONS

Available in a wide range of widths and materials, ribbons can be easily appliqué stitched down or applied with a running or backstitch. Silk ribbons are the most adaptable as they have a soft texture and are not as stiff as synthetic types. You can use silk ribbons to create loops, pleats and textures. Ribbons could also be used to finish off a raw edge of a fabric, much like the cord applied on pages 65–67.

CORDS

You can make your own cords using a cord winder, as demonstrated on pages 68–69. Doing so allows you to coordinate the threads you use with your appliqué work. When making cords I use stranded embroidery cottons. Cords can also be purchased ready-made and are sewn down with an invisible stitch. Cords work well to conceal raw fabric edges.

BEADS AND SEQUINS

When you are working a small area, beads and sequins can be used to create wonderful effects. There is a wide range of beads available, from tiny seed beads up to long bugle beads. Sometimes I will substitute sequins for a 'spangle', which is a metal version of a sequin. Shisha mirrors are also useful in embroidery where you require a reflective surface area larger than a sequin.

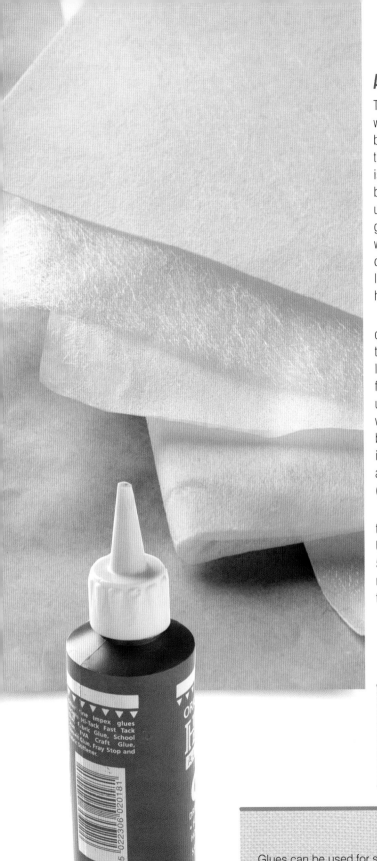

ADHESIVES

There are many different iron-on adhesives suitable for appliqué work. They are constructed from an ultra-thin sheet of adhesive that is backed with iron-resistant paper. The adhesive melts when ironed to the reverse of the fabric being applied. Once the iron-resistant paper is removed and the piece is placed on the ground fabric, the iron can be applied again to fuse the appliqué piece in place. Baking paper is useful when fusing materials together as it will prevent any adhesive getting stuck to the iron. Most adhesives are produced in different weights and you should choose the weight according to the density of the material you are applying. For example, a silk would require a light or medium adhesive, whereas a thicker fabric would require a heavier adhesive.

When working on a flat area without padding, fusible web is a quick and easy way to adhere a fabric (see page 56). For lightweight to medium-weight fabrics, and when hand stitching edges, use a lightweight or medium-weight fusible web. If you are using a heavy fabric, such as cord or velvet, a heavyweight fusible web can be used as it is a stronger adhesive. However, remember when working with a heavy fusible web that it can be rather tough to stitch through by hand, so consider machine sewing the edges of your fabric instead. Fusible web adhesives such as Bondaweb, Vilene, Mistifuse and Heat and Bond create a secure bond and prevent edges fraying (see page 15).

Freezer paper is useful for appliqué as it has a shiny plastic side that is fusible when ironed and allows you to shape fabric pieces. Usually freezer paper is used for needle-turned appliqué (see pages 58–59). Adhesives cannot be used on felted, padded areas as they do not stick well to the felt and, due to the crisp nature of the adhesive, the fabric will not sit smoothly on a raised area.

21

Protecting your iron

When working with fusible web adhesives, place baking paper on top of the fabric to prevent the glue melting onto your iron.

Using glues

Glues can be used for stabilising fabric edges. Fabrics that are tricky to use in appliqué are generally those with a high pile or that have a relatively open weave. When working with fabrics that fray easily such as velvets, cord or damask, use a product such as Fray Check, which prevents fraying on the raw edges of the fabric. Alternatively, use a conservation glue or a product called 'tacky glue', which can be watered down for using on fabrics and is quick drying.

GETTING STARTED

Lightweight background fabrics will need to be applied to a calico (muslin) or linen base to stabilise them before stitching. If you are working in a small circular frame, this step is done first; when working on a larger slate frame this is done once the calico (muslin) or linen is framed up (see pages 24–29).

TENSIONING YOUR FABRIC

It is important to tension both fabrics so that neither are over-stretched and so that they sit flat together. Both pieces of fabric should be cut square so that the grain lines are consistent. The backing fabric of either calico (muslin) or linen should be cut 2.5cm (1in) larger all round than the fabric you are applying. You will secure the layers together with a herringbone stitch using a double thread, so that both layers have some movement in them and are not completely locked.

Creating
a contrast

All the stitches in the techniques have been demonstrated using a contrasting thread so that the photographs are clear. In most cases you would choose a toning thread that sits with the fabric or edging you are applying, unless the contrast is a deliberate design feature.

22

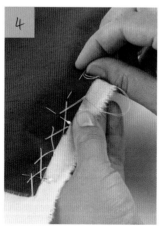

1 Keep the fabrics flat on the table as you work. Pin the two layers together. Place a pin in the middle of each side of the fabric; pin one side, then pin the opposite side, then repeat.

2 Continue placing pins roughly 2.5cm (1in) apart. Work from the middle outwards, and again, pin one side, then turn the fabric to pin the opposite side out.

3 Thread up a double length of machine thread and cast on at the edge of the calico (muslin) with a knot and two waste stitches, then cut off the knot (see page 39). Your thread will be on the top of the fabric. Scoop the needle through the purple background fabric to create the first part of the herringbone stitch.

4 Pull the needle through, then scoop back through the calico (muslin) at the very edge of the purple fabric. Continue to stitch in the same way to secure the two fabrics together.

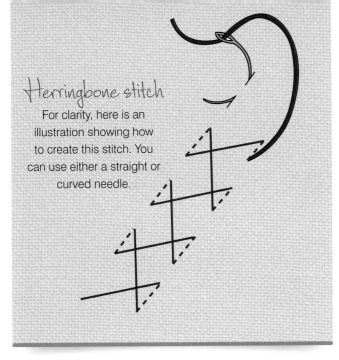

Herringbone stitch

For clarity, here is an illustration showing how to create this stitch. You can use either a straight or curved needle.

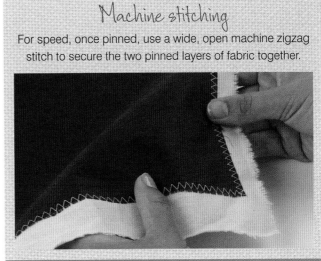

Machine stitching

For speed, once pinned, use a wide, open machine zigzag stitch to secure the two pinned layers of fabric together.

FRAMING UP A RING FRAME

To achieve a tight tension to your ring frame, both pieces are traditionally wrapped in bias binding or calico (muslin) strips. Ensure that the two pieces fit snugly together. Once you have secured your fabric, you will need to ensure that it is drum-tight. Keeping the fabric taut will prevent puckering and can help to keep the tension of your stitches even.

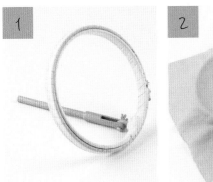
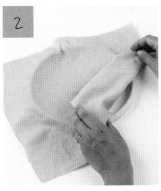
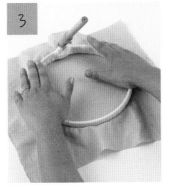

1 Wrap both of your hoops with overlapped bias binding or calico (muslin) strips. Secure the fabric at each end with a few stitches.

2 Remove the outer frame and place this on a flat surface. Lay your fabric centrally over the top of it.

3 Use two hands to press the inner hoop into the middle of the outer hoop, so that the fabric is trapped between them.

4 Adjust your fabric as necessary to ensure that it is taut. Use a screwdriver to tighten the screw at the top of the frame. Once framed up, the fabric in a ring frame should be drum-tight.

Creating grip

Rather than binding a frame with fabric you can always wrap it with plastic food wrap, as this sticks well and can be easily replaced when necessary.

FRAMING UP A SLATE FRAME

Here I will show you how to successfully frame up a slate frame. Once your fabric is secured to the calico (muslin) background, you can adjust the tension on the fabric by moving the frame's pins into different holes on the arms.

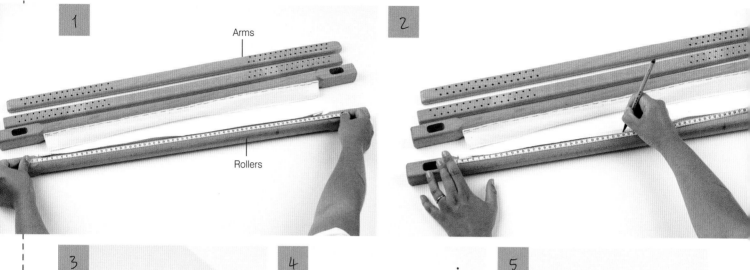

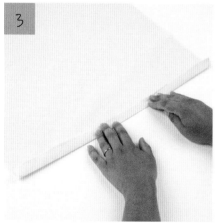

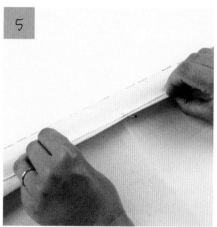

1 Slate frames are handmade, so it is not guaranteed that each roller will be the same length. Check the length of both with a tape measure before you start. Measure the distance between the two large holes.

2 Mark each roller's mid-point on the webbing using a pencil.

3 Fold over the top and bottom of the calico (muslin) backing, on the grain of the fabric, by 1.5cm (²⁄₃in).

4 To find the centre of the fabric, fold it in half and insert a glass-headed pin at this point.

5 Match the glass-headed pin to the mid-point marked on the roller, and pin the calico (muslin) to the webbing so that the folded edge sits directly underneath the webbing.

6 Pin the folded calico (muslin) edge and webbing together. Do so by working outwards from the middle of the webbing to the right-hand edge, spacing the pins 2.5cm (1in) apart, smoothing the fabric at a slight tension against the webbing.

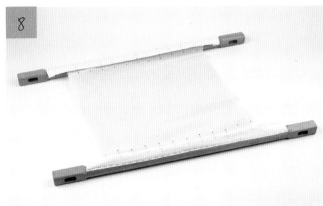

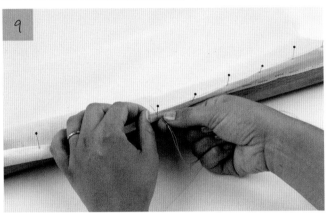

7 Return to the mid-point and then pin outwards to the left-hand edge, again spacing the pins about 2.5cm (1in) apart, attaching the calico (muslin) all the way along its length.

8 Repeat steps 4–7 on the opposite side of the roller so that each end of the calico (muslin) is pinned in place.

9 Thread a size 7 or 9 embroidery needle, or a large sharps needle, with buttonhole thread and tie a knot in the end. Starting at the mid-point, cast on the thread by making two overcast stitches, then continue the overcast stitches along towards the right-hand edge, locking both the calico (muslin) and webbing together.

10 The overcast stitches should be 3mm (⅛in) apart; alternate the lengths so that the tension is distributed evenly across the webbing. Varying the stitch size prevents the fabric ripping when the frame is tightened. Remove the glass-headed pins as you sew.

11 To finish off the thread at the edge of the calico (muslin), work several stitches overlapping those you have already done and then cut off the buttonhole thread.

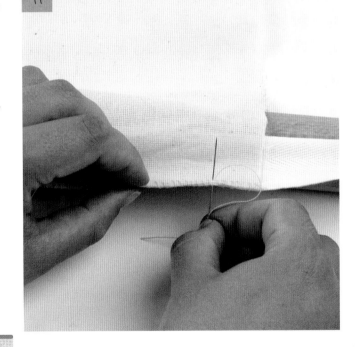

Cutting your background fabric

Make sure it is cut on the grain of the fabric so that the length and width are the same at both ends of the fabric. This will ensure an even tension to work on across your frame.

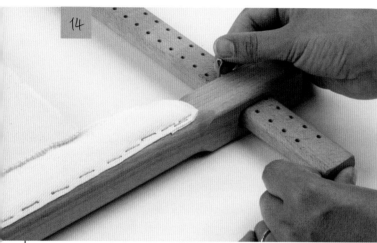

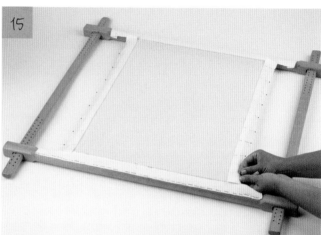

12 Return to the mid-point and sew outwards to the left-hand edge this time, using overcast stitch and buttonhole thread. Repeat steps 9–11 on the opposite roller; the calico (muslin) is now securely attached.

13 Slot the arms into the frame. Make sure each arm is a mirror image to each other so that the holes in the arms are in the same place.

14 Insert the split pins or pegs into the holes to hold the rollers away from each other and to tighten the calico (muslin). The fabric should be tight but not drum-tight at this stage.

15 Pin a strip of cotton webbing, otherwise known as herringbone tape, to both unstitched edges of the calico (muslin) so that it sits evenly along the grain of the fabric. Two-thirds of the webbing should be on the fabric and the other one-third should be off the fabric.

16 Thread a size 7–9 embroidery needle, or large sharps needle, with buttonhole thread and knot the end. Make two stitches through the calico (muslin) and webbing at the top of the frame, then cut the knot off. Work a diagonal stitch that is roughly 2cm (¾in) long through the webbing and up under the edge of the calico (muslin), pulling it firm as you go so that the webbing folds over the edge of the calico (muslin). When you reach the other end of the frame, cast off the buttonhole thread with two additional stitches. Repeat this process on the other side of the calico (muslin) so that both pieces of webbing are attached.

17 With your fabric secured, place the frame onto a trestle so that you can string it. Thread the end of a ball of string into an upholstery bracing needle. Starting at the top of one edge, take the needle down into the edge of the webbing – being careful not to insert it through the calico (muslin). Create stitches by coming up around the arm of the frame with the string every 2.5cm (1in). Once completed, cut the string leaving a 50cm (20in) tail on each end. Repeat this process on the other side of the frame.

18 Slacken off the frame by taking the split pins out of the arms and placing them in holes further towards the middle of the frame. Take your background fabric – here I have used purple silk – and lay this onto the calico (muslin) so that it sits in the same direction with the grains of both fabrics matching.

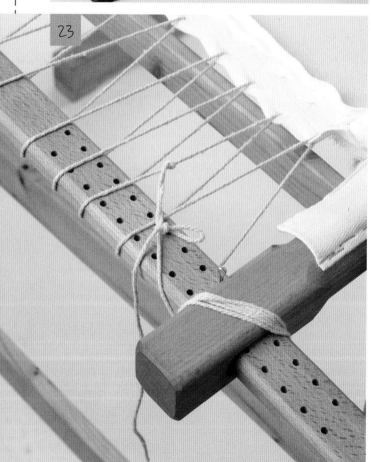

19 Place a pin through both layers of fabric, in the middle of each side, pinning one side then the opposite side, then repeating for the other two sides.

20 Continue placing pins roughly 2.5cm (1in) apart, working from the middle out, pinning one side in place and then turning the fabric around to ease the opposite side out.

21 Thread a needle with a doubled length of machine thread. Cast on at the edge of the calico (muslin) with a knot and two waste stitches, then cut the knot off. Scoop the needle through the purple silk for the first part of the herringbone stitch, then return to the calico (muslin) for the next stitch.

22 Continue to work this stitch around all four edges of the purple silk fabric. Remove the pins once the fabric is stitched.

23 Apply some more tension to the frame by moving the split pins further out from the middle of the frame; move them one by one, to increase the tension evenly.

Pinning out fabric

Both fabrics should lie flat and at the same tension. If puckers form in the fabric you are applying, you are pinning too tightly against the calico (muslin).

24 You now need to tighten the tension on the string. Starting from the centre of the right-hand strip of webbing, work towards one edge, pulling the string tight and adjusting all the loops. Secure the string with a slip knot at one end and then return to the middle of the webbing and work back in the opposite direction. You are aiming for the webbing edge to sit perpendicular to the arm of the frame so that the calico (muslin) is evenly stretched. Once one side of the frame is tensioned, tighten the opposite side using the same method.

25 To tension the frame so that it is drum-tight, stand the base of the frame upright on the floor and use the sole of your foot to push down the end of the bottom roller so that the split pin can be pulled out. Push down again to move the pin into a lower hole so that the tension on the fabric is increased. Repeat on the opposite side so that both split pins sit within the same corresponding holes, to give even tension across the frame. To doublecheck that the frame is at a consistent tension, measure the distance between the rollers at each side of the frame.

The framed-up fabric.

DESIGN

The design stage is fundamental. Careful planning will help you
to create a smooth and well-balanced piece of appliqué.

COMPOSING A DESIGN

It is wise to take your time at the design stage: although it is possible
to adjust certain aspects or elements of your design as you work on it,
by and large, appliqué tends to work most successfully if you create a
thorough plan and then stick to it. For the design stage you will need
your initial idea, pencils, tracing paper and a photocopier to speed
up the design process. When I work I always start with my own idea,
usually in the form of a photograph or a sketch that has inspired me.

Consider the composition of your design: do you want to isolate
a section of your inspirational photograph or sketch and work this,
or do you want to work the whole piece? Perhaps lines of the design
need to be extended so that the design is asymmetric and a little
more playful, or maybe certain elements need to be excluded or
enlarged. Think of your embroidery as a piece of art – the viewer will
interpret the piece in differing ways according to its composition. Use
the tracing paper to create a sketch of the overall design – only draw
out the elements of your design you want to include, and mix up the
spacing, sizing and layout to suit your taste.

Look at your drawn tracing critically. If any elements are confusing
or don't read well, you might need to take them out or re-design
certain areas. Think of this stage as though you were taking a
snapshot of your design and looking at it objectively – often when
you take a photograph, not everything is represented as you might
think. Consider also that designs for appliqué are usually not overly
intricate, as shapes need to be of fair size in order to turn under
fabric edges. Smaller details are often replicated through embroidery
stitches. When looking at your design, consider what techniques you
want to use as at this point, before you begin to cut or sew any fabrics
– you may need to scale up a design to make shapes easier to handle
or even reject a design and think of another. Once you have decided
what techniques you want to use for each element of your design, you
will need to work out an order of work (see pages 32–33).

USING COLOUR

Having an understanding of colour will help you with design as it
makes you consider what you are trying to achieve. My work is quite
bold and I often achieve this by using bright colours. To make colours
really zing I would use complementary colours: reds and greens,
blues and oranges or purples and yellows. For a softer effect, putting
colours together that sit next to each other in the colour wheel works
very well – these are called analogous colours. For example, in my
Poppy project (see pages 94–102) I have used a deep purple velvet
background and combined this with orange-red petals, as purples,
reds and oranges sit next to each other in the colour wheel. Colour
tones within fabrics are a measure of how much dye something
contains – when working with colours it can be worth doing a black
and white copy of your design to see how much light is in each of
the colours within the design. Bear in mind also that sometimes
monotone designs can look really effective; see page 41 for an
example of where one colour is used in varying tones.

CHOOSING FABRICS AND THREADS

Once you have refined your design you are now ready to have a dig
through your box of fabrics and select which ones work well for your
design – or even better, perhaps purchase some new fabrics to add
to your stash! When selecting, think about the play of light and texture
and how all the fabrics look as a whole together.

When selecting threads to use within your piece, the tone of the
thread is usually denoted by the last number on its cuff so if you wish
to use similar tones of thread, use similar numbers. For a more bright
and eye-catching design take threads from differing ends of the range
to create more contrast (see page 20 for further inspiration).

'Appliqué work is thought to be an inferior kind of
embroidery, which it is not. It is not a lower but another kind of
needlework, in which more is made of the stuff than the stitching. In it the craft of the
needleworker is not carried to its limit; but, on the other hand, it makes great demands upon design.
You cannot begin by just throwing about sprays of natural flowers. It calls peremptorily for treatment –
by which test the decorative artist stands or falls. Effective it must be, vulgar it should not be, trivial it can
hardly be; mere prettiness is beyond its scope; and it lends itself to dignity of design and nobility of treatment.'

Lewis Day, *Art in Needlework*

ORDER OF WORK

Once you are happy with the size and style of your design, trace the outlines to create a simple line drawing, and photocopy it. 'Fill in' the different areas of the design on the photocopy, noting which techniques you want to use where. Once you have decided which technique will be most successful for each area, you will need to create an order-of-work – either on the techniques sheet or on a separate photocopy – to follow during the stitching process, starting with the background of the design first and working towards the foreground elements. Here are a few things to consider when planning the order of your work.

TRANSLATING YOUR DESIGN

You will need to start by transferring your design onto your background fabric. When working appliqué there are several different ways to translate a design onto your background fabric: you can use the traditional prick and pounce method, use a light box and pencil or paint, create templates or work a straight tacking stitch (see pages 34–37).

MACHINE FIRST

If you want to include some machine work in your design and you plan to use a slate frame, machine any areas in the background and complete any fusible web appliqué prior to framing up. Otherwise, the slate frame's mechanics will get in the way of the sewing machine. Once machining is complete, you can then frame up the background fabric and tighten the frame.

USING THE GRAIN

Ensure that when you position your fabric, you apply it so that it sits straight with the grain of the background fabric. Applying a piece of fabric on the bias will give it more stretch and it will not handle in the same way so it makes sense to keep it consistent across the piece, unless it is done for effect and to achieve folds and undulations in the fabric.

ADJUSTING YOUR TENSION

When applying fabrics, think about adjusting your frame tension prior to applying each different material, as this will make the end result smoother. If you are building up padded, raised areas, some of the first fabrics to consider will be felt and carpet felt. These will need to be worked on a tight frame, as they have no stretch. When working felt, consider which areas sit flatter and complete these first, then work the higher relief areas. When appliquéing fabrics, you will need to use a looser frame. Slacken the frame off a little so that the tension of the frame is similar to that of the fabric you are applying. For example, if you are applying a fine silk you will need to loosen your frame more than if you are applying a cotton.

BACK TO FRONT

Fabrics should be applied to the design starting with the background and working towards the foreground. Usually if fabrics are not adhered to the surface with an adhesive they will need pinning then tacking to get them to sit flat. Smaller elements of appliqué fabric can be tacked in place with a straight tacking stitch but larger pieces should be secured with a diagonal tacking stitch to ease them out so they are the same tension as the calico (muslin) fabric across the whole piece and without any wrinkles. It is especially important to diagonally tack fabrics that sit on top of padding so that the fabric remains smooth. These stitches are not decorative and will be removed once all the fabrics are stitched down.

Once each appliqué piece is tacked down, you will stitch it down, either using a needle-turned edge or with appliqué stitch (see pages 48–51). You will then complete each piece with edging stitches to conceal the appliqué stitches (see pages 60–67). For dense edging stitches such as satin stitch and long and short stitch, once you have tacked your fabric in place it is wise to do an appliqué stitch first, as this prevents the fabric from shifting and puckering.

For any fabrics that are heavily embroidered or that sit with embroidery on top of heavy padding, it is advisable to work the embroidery on a ring frame and then apply it to the main frame once the background areas are secured. If you are unsure about any processes, or the effect that you will achieve, you should sample them first prior to committing them to the main frame.

33

All my work comes from drawings I have done or photographs I have taken so that each piece is truly my own work. When looking at a design, I initially think about which techniques would work best and in considering this, I think about scale and which techniques are most suitable to specific areas. Once I have techniques in mind, I then trace off the design areas onto tracing paper and then list where I would start on the design, working from the background to the foreground, and noting which techniques sit in individual areas. This is referred to as an order of work.

TRANSFERRING YOUR DESIGN

When creating an appliqué piece there are a few different ways that you can translate a design onto your background fabric. You can use the traditional prick and pounce method, use a light box and pencil, pen or paint, create templates or use tacking stitches.

PRICK AND POUNCE METHOD

This is the traditional method of transferring a design. It has been used for centuries and gives you total precision, as your design is perforated and translated directly onto the fabric; it is ideal if you want to repeat the pattern, as a pricking can be used many times. This method of transferring a design is especially useful when working with dark fabrics or fabrics with a heavy pile that you cannot see through to use with a lightbox.

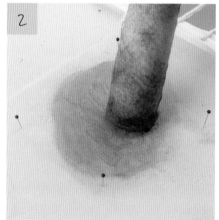

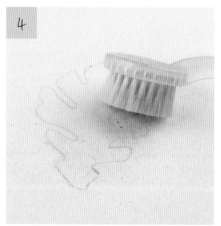

1 Once your design is traced off onto tracing paper, place the tracing onto a thick layer of fabric, or a towel, and place a size 9 embroidery needle into your pricker. Prick holes through the tracing that are about 2mm (¹⁄₁₆in) apart.

2 Pin the pricking to the fabric on your frame and then rub pounce (ground charcoal) through the perforated design lines using a pounce brush (see tip box, below).

3 Take out the pins and lift the pricking off the fabric. Tip any excess pounce off the pricking into a jar to be used again. Take a sharp H propelling pencil and join the dots to recreate your design on the fabric.

4 Turn the frame over and pat the back firmly to remove any excess pounce powder. If necessary, brush off any excess pounce with a baby brush or face brush.

Making your own brush
A pounce brush – used to apply pounce – can be made from rolled soft felt or a domette fabric.

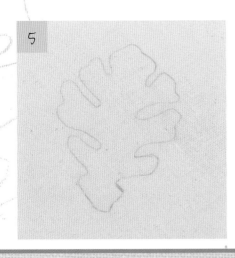

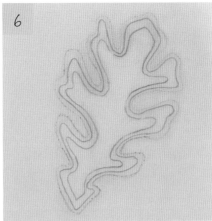

5 The design is now translated onto the fabric ready for padding.

6 Once you clean up your pricking you can use it again. I added two inner lines to the leaf shape – these indicate the raised areas I will create later in felt – I will either use them as further pricking lines or they will be photocopied as templates for my felt.

Did you know...

Traditionally ground cuttlefish was used for dark fabrics and ground charcoal for light fabrics. Ground chalk can also be used for dark fabrics.

USING PAINT

Once you have pounced the design onto fabric you can then paint over the dots to recreate your design. It is traditional to use tubed watercolour paint or oils. Avoid acrylics and gouache as they are not as successful on fabrics.

Choosing your brush

Use a really fine paintbrush to create smooth delicate lines – I use a 000 brush size.

1 Prick and pounce your design, as shown opposite. Remove the pricking from the fabric to reveal the pounce line.

2 Using slightly diluted watercolour, which should have the consistency of unwhipped double cream, paint over the pounce dots using a fine paintbrush to create a smooth consistent line.

USING A LIGHTBOX

This method is quick and successful for fine, lightweight and light-coloured fabrics.

1 Tape your design onto the lightbox. Tape the fabric on top of the design to prevent it slipping.

2 Trace off the design with a sharp H pencil.

Darkening your design
If you cannot see your design through the lightbox, try re-tracing it with a black pen.

USING A TEMPLATE

You can use templates for appliqué once you have your design line drawing completed. If you photocopy this several times you can cut pieces into paper template shapes. When using this method it is worth having some design reference lines either as tack lines or drawn or painted on the fabric ground to help you with placement. If your shape is irregular, cut the design out leaving a border of about 5mm (¼in). Cut out and then snip into this allowance so that the fabric edge will turn under easily.

1 When drawing out your template, add a 5mm (¼in) allowance around the entire shape; this will be your seam allowance. Pin your template to the right side of your fabric.

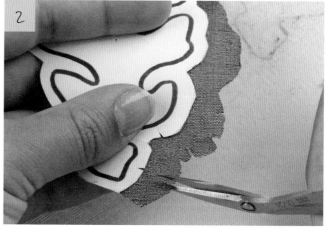

2 Cut out the fabric around the template. Cut notches into the curves of the seam allowance, every 5mm (¼in) or so.

USING TISSUE PAPER

This technique can be used if you are not accurate with a paintbrush or pencil, or when using fabrics with a pile, which are harder to paint smooth design lines onto.

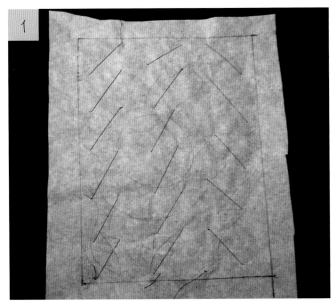

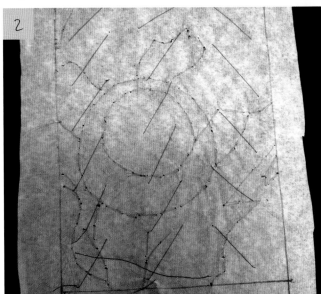

Making a clear guide
When tacking on your design, keep your stitches small on the reverse and larger on the front so that you have a clearer design line to follow.

1 Trace off the design onto tissue paper and pin this to your fabric. Tack the tissue paper to the fabric with diagonal tacking stitches through the middle of the design in rows and create a few more lines of stitches out towards the edges of the design so that the tissue paper lies flat.

2 Using a machine thread with a knot in its tail, start the tail on the surface of the tissue paper and work a running stitch from the middle of the design working your way to the outer edges so the design is smoothed out. To cast off the thread, bring the needle up to the surface and tie a knot to secure the thread.

3 When the design lines are all stitched, remove the diagonal tacking stitches and tear the tissue paper away from the fabric to reveal the design lines. If the tissue gets stuck in the stitches, remove it with tweezers.

Straight tacking and diagonal tacking
Although similar, straight and diagonal tacking stitches have slightly different uses. I would use straight tacking stitches on small fabric shapes and for securing turned edges. Diagonal tacking stitch should be used to secure larger fabric shapes or tissue designs on top of fabric.

Left, diagonal tacking.

Below, straight tacking.

ESSENTIAL STARTING TECHNIQUES

Here are a few very basic techniques to get you started. It is crucial to knot your thread and then start stitching in a secure way, to ensure that your stitches do not come undone in the future.

THREADING A NEEDLE

Take your thread between your thumb and index finger so that less than 2mm (¹/₁₆in) of the thread is showing. Holding the needle with your dominant hand, push the needle onto the thread.

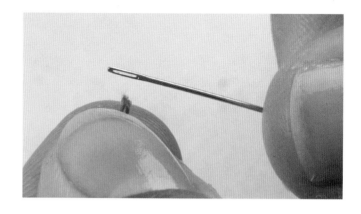

TYING A KNOT

This is the easiest way to put a knot into the end of your thread.

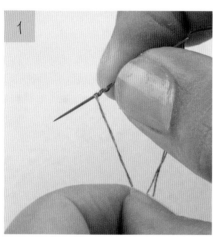

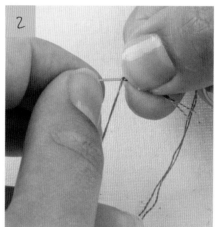

1 Thread your needle. Using your thumb and index finger, hold the tail onto the shaft of the needle so that the tail is at the eye end. Wrap the thread two or three times around the needle towards the sharp end of the needle.

2 Hold the wrapped loops on the needle with your dominant thumb.

3 Pull the needle through.

4 You have a knotted thread.

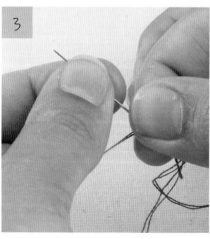

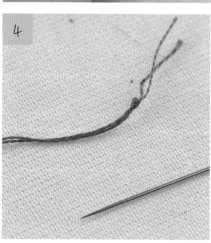

Pulling through

If you are struggling to pull your needle through at step 3, don't hold the loops around the needle quite so tightly. Having a softer tension should allow you to pull the needle through with less resistance.

CASTING ON

This is one of the most fundamental rules of embroidery. When working professionally, casting on and casting off is always done on the front of the frame and waste knots are cut off so that they do not get in the way of subsequent stitches. You should always cast on and cast off near to your first or last stitch so that there is not a long stitch on the reverse of the frame, as this can affect the fabric tension.

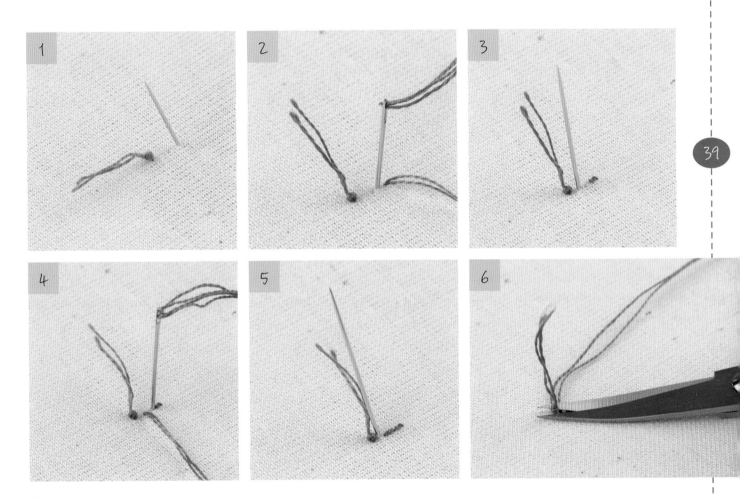

1 Make a knot in the end of the thread. Take the needle down through the fabric and then bring it up in front of the knot.

2 Work a small backstitch that is roughly 1mm (1/16in) long.

3 Bring up the needle between the first stitch and the knot.

4 Create another 1mm (1/16in) backstitch that goes back down into the hole of the first stitch created.

5 Come up at the starting point of your second stitch.

6 Cut the waste knot off on the surface of the fabric.

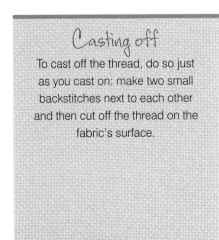

Casting off

To cast off the thread, do so just as you cast on: make two small backstitches next to each other and then cut off the thread on the fabric's surface.

PRINCIPLES OF BUILDING UP

When applying or building up layers of padding it is important to have a tight frame as felt has no stretch – a tight frame will help to prevent any padding distorting the background fabric on the reverse of the frame. There are four main ways of building up a design, two of which can be done from the front of the frame, by creating layers of padding, and the other two are done by forcing soft pliable padding either just behind a slip or by cutting and stuffing through the calico (muslin) base layer. You can also create relief in small areas using padded satin stitch (see pages 120–121 for this).

In my Poppy project (shown above) I used a carpet felt circle to create the protruding centre of the poppy (see pages 94–102).

FELT PADDING

This is the most common type of padding: layers of felt are cut to build up relief to the desired level. The first piece of felt is always the smallest and sits within the design area. Gradually, larger pieces of felt are applied to eventually fill up to the design line. Carpet felt allows you to build up high reliefs in large areas. The carpet felt is cut to the size of the shape you are padding, stitched down and then subsequent smaller layers are added. You will need to add a final layer of felt for a smooth surface.

STRING PADDING

This technique is useful for padding areas that are 1cm (½in) or less wide. It forms a strong foundation onto which fabrics, including leather kid, can be applied. The string can be tapered down from a high level to a low level, so this technique works well for undulations in relief.

In my Fern project (shown below) I used felt and carpet felt padding to create raised interest (see pages 72–79).

SLIP PADDING

You would create a slip on a separate frame and then apply it to the main frame. Once the slip is partially sewn down you should then take a wad of toy stuffing or broken-up wadding (batting), cotton wool, kapok or fleece and push this behind the slip with a pair of tweezers to fill the area. Once the area is filled, the slip can then be sewn down completely.

TRUPUNTO PADDING

Here you will cut the foundation fabrics that sit behind the slip and stuff using toy stuffing, broken-up wadding (batting), kapok or fleece from the reverse of the frame. Once the slip is stuffed, you will overcast the hole using a curved needle (see page 47).

40

Narnia
30 x 19cm (12 x 7½in)
Auburn Claire Lucas

A scene from C. S. Lewis's fictional Narnia – from *The Lion, the Witch and the Wardrobe* – created
in white cotton, organza and silk, with a hand-painted sky. A combination of finished edges is used,
including corded, frayed, couched, satin and split stitch, with a stumpwork umbrella.

PADDING: LAYERING UP

USING FELT

This is the most common type of padding: layers of felt are cut to build up relief to the desired level. The first piece of felt is always the smallest and sits within the design area. Gradually pieces of felt get larger to eventually fill the space up to the design line on the background fabric.

Working on large areas

If you are securing a large area of felt it is sensible to put a few initial appliqué stitches in on all sides, so that the piece is secure and cannot shift around. Once these are in place, work the appliqué stitches 4mm (³/₁₆in) apart as usual.

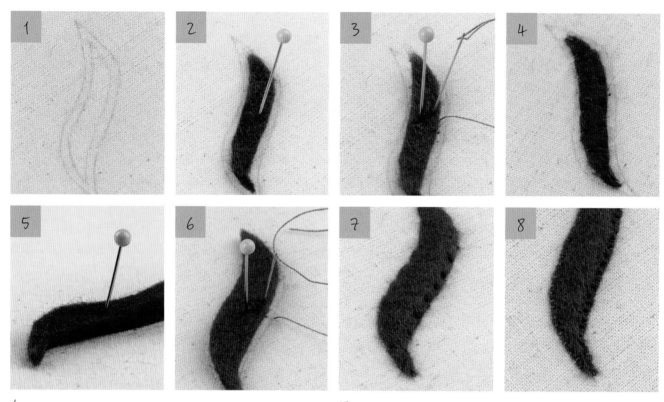

1 Pounce on the outer design and where the first layer of felt should sit within the shape.

2 Using your pricking, pouce this onto the felt and then cut the felt 2mm (¹/₁₆in) inside the pounce line to form the first smallest layer of felt.

3 Cast on using machine thread and a small embroidery needle (see page 39). I use a size 10 but a larger size would work too. Create an appliqué stitch by coming up in the background fabric and bringing the needle down in the felt. The stitch should be about 2mm (¹/₁₆in) long. Continue to work appliqué stitch around the edge of the shape, spacing the stitches about 4mm (³/₁₆in) apart.

4 Put stitches in the tips of the shape. Cast off with two stitches once you have worked the appliqué stitches back to where you started.

5 Pounce outline of the second design shape onto your felt – this should fit to the edge of your design line area. Cut the piece of felt out and secure it with a pin.

6 Create an appliqué stitch by coming up in the background fabric on the design line and taking the stitch back down into the felt. The stitch should be about 2mm (¹/₁₆in) long. Continue to work appliqué stitch around the edge of the shape, spacing the stitches about 4mm (³/₁₆in) apart.

7 Continue in the same way until you get back to the start. Ensure that you put stitches into the tips, so that the entire shape is secure.

8 Work the whole way around the shape again, inserting two stitches between each that you have already worked so that the stitches are now about 2mm (¹/₁₆in) apart.

USING CARPET FELT

Carpet felt is used when high relief is required as it is equivalent to five layers of regular felt. The carpet felt should be cut to the size of the shape you are padding, stitched down and then subsequent smaller layers can be added for further height. The final layer should be covered with a piece of felt to give a smooth surface. When working a shape with different heights in design, always work the lower level piece first. In this design I worked the single layer of blue felt prior to working the higher carpet felt leaf turnover. For the clarity of photography, in this technique and throughout the book, I have used fewer pins than normal. When working, you should use enough pins to hold the piece securely.

Avoiding distortion

It is particularly important to have a tight tension on your fabric when using carpet felt, to prevent the felt distorting the reverse of the background fabric.

43

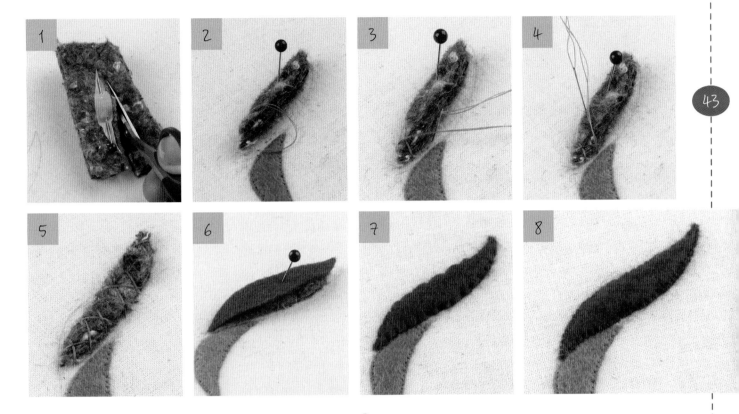

1 Use your design template to cut a piece of carpet felt. The piece should be 2mm ($^1/_{16}$in) smaller all the way around than the design area it is to fill.

2 Secure the carpet felt with a pin. Thread a needle with a doubled length of machine thread and cast on (see page 39). Take a herringbone stitch across the carpet felt at a diagonal angle.

3 Come up beside where you have taken the needle down to begin creating a herringbone stitch that oversews the carpet felt to the background fabric.

4 Take the needle down on the opposite side.

5 Continue to work herringbone stitch up the entire length of the shape, then cast off the thread.

6 Pounce the design shape onto the felt and cut this out – it should exactly fill the design area. Secure the felt in position with a pin.

7 Work an appliqué stitch around the entire edge of the felt shape. The stitches should be about 2mm ($^1/_{16}$in) long and about 4mm ($^3/_{16}$in) apart.

8 Work two further appliqué stitches in between those you have already worked so that the stitches are now about 2mm ($^1/_{16}$in) apart. Cast off with two stitches once you get back to the starting stitch.

Applying large pieces of felt

For large areas of carpet felt that only require one layer, you will need to put more pins in initially to position the piece. It can be worth starting your overcast herringbone stitch in the middle and working out one way, then returning back to the middle and working in the other directon. This will ensure the felt is completely smoothed and fills the area snugly. See page 45 for padding large, complex shapes with carpet felt.

STRING PADDING

Soft cotton or 'Bumf' (see glossary on page 128) is used for goldwork in areas narrow in design but can also be used in appliqué where you have a highly padded narrow area with fabric or leather on top. If you cannot source Bumf then a stranded cotton or soft cotton would work just as well. String padding is always worked from the widest point of the design so that string can be cut away and reduced towards tapered points.

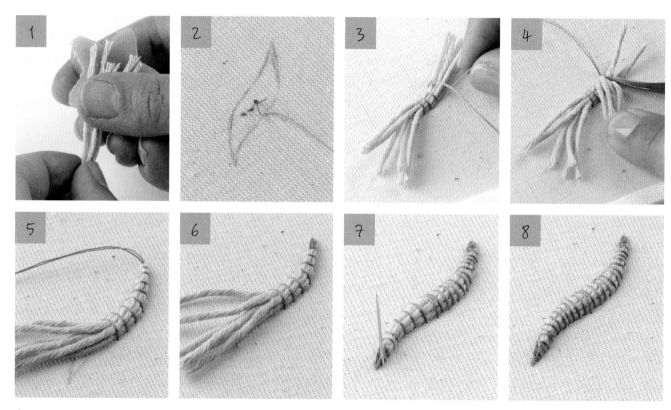

1 Wax your string with beeswax to make the thread more pliable and so that the string bundle will stick together.

2 Cast on with a double machine thread with two 1mm (¹/₁₆in) backstitches and then cut off the knot.

3 Starting at the widest point of the design area, which in this case is the middle of the shape, work couching stitches over the string at 2mm (¹/₁₆in) intervals towards the top of the shape.

4 As the shape narrows, cut away individual strings from the bottom of the set after each couching stitch so that the quantity of string reduces as the shape tapers to a point.

5 Once you have reached the point of the shape, come up with the needle at the very tip.

6 Work some stitches in varying sizes back into the tip of the string to prevent fraying.

7 Return back to the middle of the shape by working couching stitches in between the initial couching. Then at the middle continue 2mm (¹/₁₆in) spaced couching stitches towards the bottom tip of the shape, cutting the string from underneath again as the shape reduces to a point. Once you have reached the bottom point again put some stitches into the string at the very point to prevent fraying.

8 Return to the middle of the shape, placing couching stitches in between the initial stitches so that all the stitches are now 1mm (¹/₁₆in) apart across the whole shape.

Working rounded shapes

When working shapes with a rounded point, you will need to cut the string to shape to fit within the area. Further stitches into the string will also be required as there is a wider area for fraying.

BUILDING UP COMPLEX SHAPES WITH CARPET FELT

Carpet felt can be used to build up complex domed shapes – create layers in decreasing sizes and secure them one at a time with herringbone stitch.

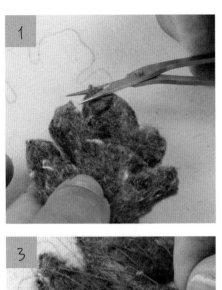

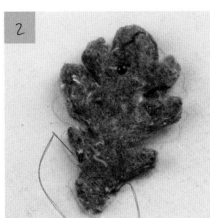

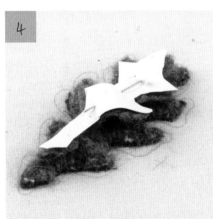

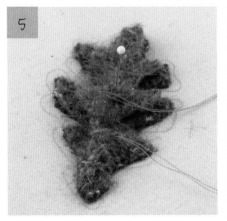

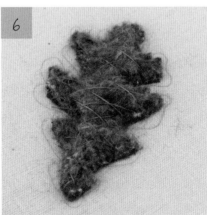

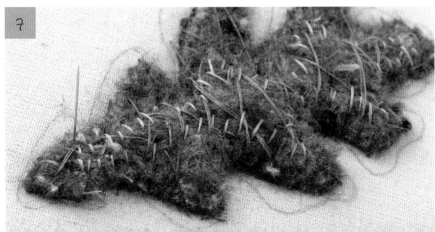

1 Cut the carpet felt so that it is 2mm (1/16in) smaller than the outer design area. Chamfer the felt edges to avoid a sudden drop in height.

2 Secure the carpet felt with a pin. Thread a needle with a doubled length of machine thread and cast on (see page 39). Take a herringbone stitch across the carpet felt at a diagonal angle. Continue the herringbone stitch all the way to the top and then cast off. Where carpet felt is especially large, a herringbone stitch will not secure the felt down. In this case, where shapes are larger than around 5cm (2in) across, use lots of pins to initially secure the felt to fabric and then long and short stitch around the outer edge of the felt.

3 Sew a long and short stitch around the entire edge of the shape – bring the needle up in the background fabric and take it back down in the edge of the felt.

4 Using a template, cut a smaller piece of carpet felt that is chamfered on the edges to avoid a sudden drop in height.

5 Pin this second felt layer in place. Stitch it directly above the first layer of felt using an oversewn herringbone stitch.

6 Your completed herringbone stitch should look like this. I have used a contrasting thread colour so that the stitching is clearly visible.

7 To ensure that the top layer is secure, work straight stitches of various lengths around the edge of the felt. Do so by coming up in the fabric and going down into the carpet felt. This stitch will secure the soft loose edge of the carpet felt. Once the carpet felt is complete, top it with a final layer of felt (see page 43).

SLIP PADDING

A slip is a piece of embroidery that is worked off the main frame and then applied to it. Slips are useful when you wish to have a large amount of detail represented in embroidery stitches. Slips can be created independently and then applied to padding so that embroidery stitches do not have to be worked through multiple layers of padding – working embroidery stitches through multiple layers causes padding and fabric distortion and often frayed fabric edges.

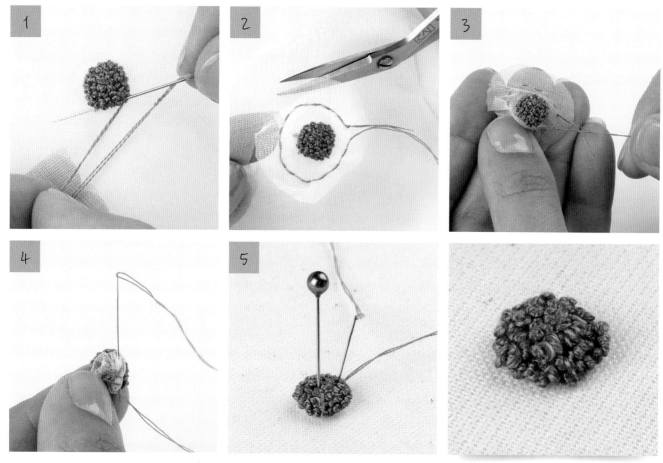

The completed slip.

1 Create the stitches – here I used French knots – in stranded embroidery thread working from the centre outwards.

2 Thread up a needle with two strands of machine thread. Put a knot in the end of your threads and then work a running stitch approximately 5mm (¼in) from the outside of the embroidery stitches. Then cut out the fabric 5mm (¼in) from the running stitch.

3 Pull the thread to gather up the stitches so that the raw edge tucks behind the embroidery stitches.

4 Work some overcast lacing stitches from one side of the slip to the other to secure the raw edge of the fabric down.

5 Pin the slip onto the main frame and then use the attached thread and needle to create a slip stitch around the slip. If you struggle with an embroidery needle you could try substituting this with a curved needle.

Tailoring your stitching
More intricate and complex shapes will need a smaller running stitch for tighter gathers.

TRAPUNTO STUFFING

Trapunto translates from Italian to mean 'to quilt', and this stuffing technique is commonly used in quilt-making. It requires two layers of fabric and is useful when you wish to build up areas from the reverse of the fabric.

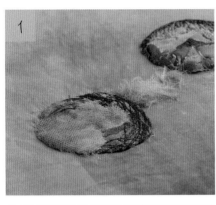 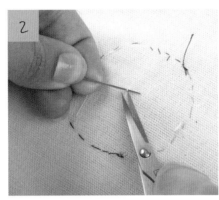 

  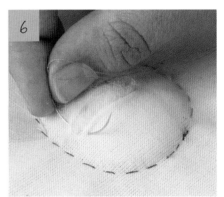

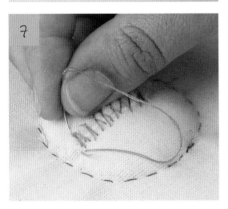 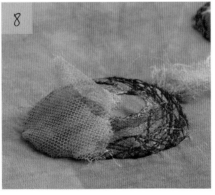

1 Apply your shape to the background: create a turned edge and stitch it down securely.

2 Turn your work over. Use a tapestry needle to lift up a few calico (muslin) threads, and snip them with a pair of sharp scissors.

3 Use your scissors to carefully snip a slit across the back of the shape, being careful to only cut the calico (muslin) fabric.

4 Carefully insert some stuffing into the hole; use tweezers or your fingers to push in the stuffing.

5 Continue to stuff until the shape is full and the fabric taut.

6 Thread a curved needle with doubled machine thread. Start to sew at one end of the slit.

7 Sew a herringbone stitch all the way across the slit and then back again, to secure.

8 From the front, your shape should look proud.

APPLYING FABRICS

When covering a felt piece or applying fabric to a flat background it is essential that fabrics are pinned and tacked down initially, before they are sewn with either a machine stitch, a slip stitch or an appliqué stitch. This preparation stage prevents the fabric from shifting and ensures a precise finish. There are two fundamental ways of applying fabrics: using an appliqué stitch or creating a needle-turned edge.

APPLIQUÉ EDGE

An appliqué stitch is an easy stitch to work and it is the same stitch that we used for applying felt (see page 42). Generally when an appliqué stitch is used it is later concealed with an overlapping embroidery stitch, cord or couching.

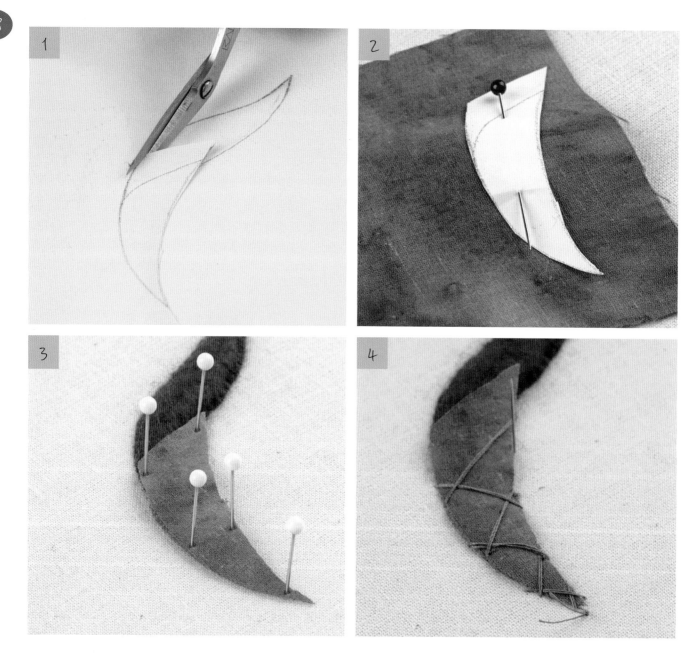

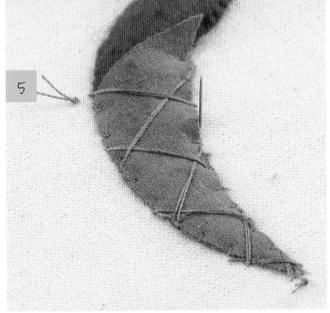

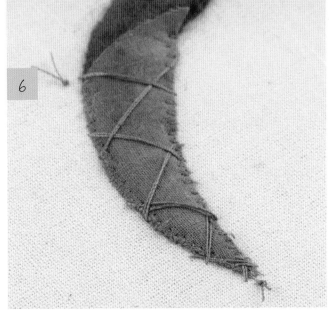

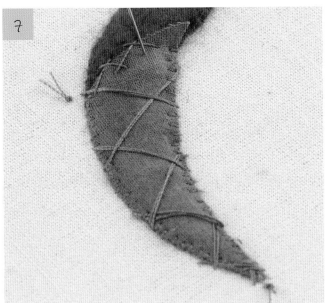

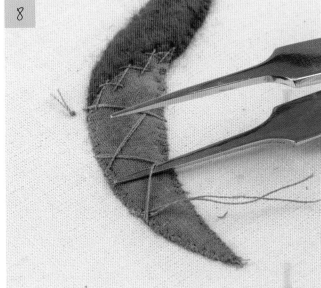

1 Cut the template from paper. In designs such as this, where you have one area overlapping another (the leaf turnover), leave a 1cm (½in) additional allowance so that the shape that sits over the top will sit without any base felt showing.

2 Pin the template to the right side of the fabric and cut it out.

3 Pin the piece of fabric to the felt.

4 Taking a doubled length of machine thread, work an overcast herringbone stitch over the shape to secure it to the felt (see page 23).

5 Cast off the machine thread using a knot on the background fabric's surface. Using one strand of machine thread, come up in the background fabric and cast on with two stitches and cut off the knot. Work appliqué stitches around the fabric edge, leaving about 4mm (³/₁₆in) gaps between stitches.

6 Work the appliqué stitch around the shape again, this time putting two new stitches between every original stitch. so that the stitches are now about 2mm (¹/₁₆in) apart.

7 Work either a small herringbone stitch in a single machine thread or a series of long and short stitches in the fabric allowance so that all sides of the fabric are secured.

8 Remove all the overcast herringbone stitch – cut through the stitches and pull the threads out with tweezers – turn your frame to the reverse to remove the cut stitches.

Removing threads

If the overcast herringbone stitches do not come out easily, make several cuts into the thread so that you do not distort the applied fabric by pulling too hard.

TURNED EDGE

A turned edge, or needle-turned appliqué, is worked so that no stitches show. Because of this, embroidery stitches, cords or couching are not required to cover or conceal the stitches. All turned edges are best worked using a single strand of machine thread. Turned edges are easiest to work on larger shapes. Where the shape of fabric is undulating or very small in size, I would use the appliqué stitch method (see pages 48–49) or machine edge the piece of fabric. When I work a turned edge, I iron the seam allowance and tack the shape down prior to completing the turned edge. Once you become adept at the technique, it will be possible to remove the tacking stage and simply turn the fabric edge under as you stitch it in place.

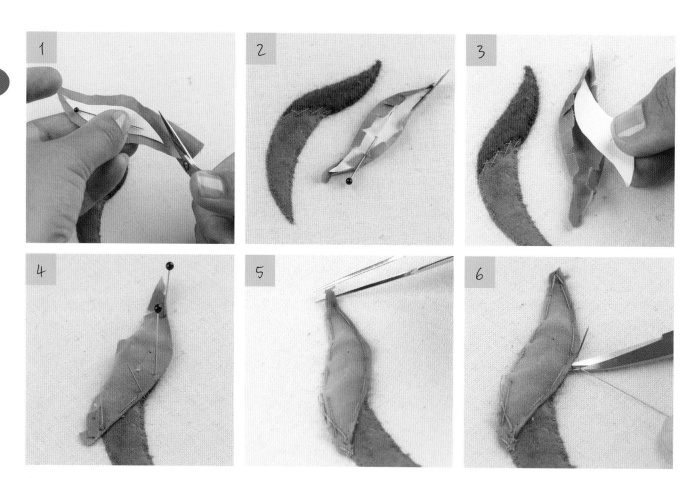

1 Pin your template to the fabric and then cut out leaving a 1cm (½in) allowance.

2 Cut notches into the fabric seams on curves, and on inner corners clip the seam allowance back to 4mm (³/₁₆in). For outer points, neatly fold one side of the allowance over the other and trim this with your scissors if bulk needs to be reduced. Once the cuts are made, press them down around the template with an iron or your fingers.

3 Remove the template from the fabric.

4 Thread up one strand of machine thread into a small embroidery needle, knot the end and tack the edges of your fabric down. Your stitches should be long on the front of the fabric and small on the reverse. Cast off the thread.

5 If points are not sitting flat use a pair of tweezers to tuck them under – if necessary put some additional tacking stitches in.

6 Thread up one strand of machine thread into a small embroidery needle. Knot the tail and then cast on with two stitches right underneath the edge of your shape, then cut off the knot so you are ready to begin the stitch.

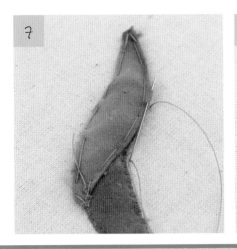

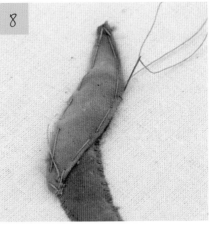

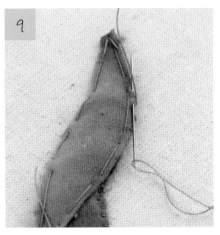

Slip stitch

Use this handy diagram to perfect your slip stitch technique.

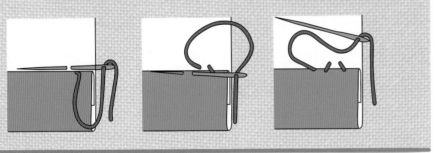

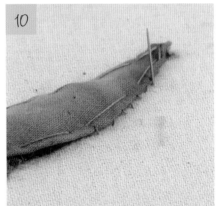

7 To create a slip stitch, bring up the needle in the background fabric as near to the fabric you are applying as possible, and scoop through 5mm (¼in) of the edge of the fabric you are applying.

8 Take the needle down into the background fabric into the calico (muslin).

9 Come up into the fabric you are applying 1mm (¹⁄₁₆in) further back from the stitch in the background fabric and then scoop through the fold by 5mm (¼in).

10 Continue working the slip stitch by alternating from the calico (muslin) background to the fabric you are applying and scooping through its fold.

11 Once you have worked three to five stitches you can then gently pull the slip stitches down so that they become invisible.

12 Complete the rest of the shape. Cut the tacking on the surface and remove it with tweezers.

Securing fabrics

I would tack down larger shapes using diagonal tacking stitches, and for a turned edge I would tack with straight tacking stitches. For larger shapes, both types can be used to smooth fabric over padding and to ensure a precise turned edge. Where fabric is applied over padding I find the overcast herringbone stitch the most useful. I do not find using pins alone successful, as appliqué pieces shift and move.

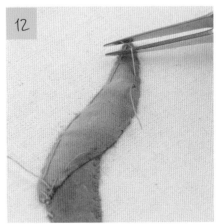

REVERSE APPLIQUÉ

In this technique, a shape is cut out from an upper layer of fabric and the seam allowance is turned under to reveal the fabric underneath. So in this instance, fabric is revealed below rather than added on top. Choose fabrics that do not fray as this technique is rather fiddly. Before working this method, fabrics should be sandwiched together: sew them together around the edge using a herringbone stitch or with a wide machine zigzag. Mola appliqué is worked using this method (see page 13).

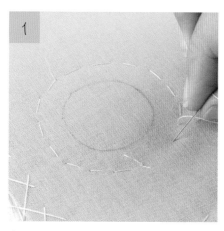  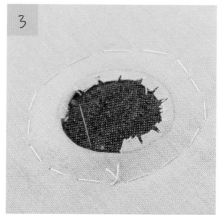

1 Once the design is marked onto the top layer of fabric, a running stitch in a single machine thread should be worked outside the seam allowance. In this example I allowed for the seam allowance to be 1cm (½in) so I tacked around the shape at 1.5cm (¾in).

2 Once the tacking is in place, lift the fabric to be cut using a tapestry needle and snip a few of the threads. Use this hole to cut out the excess central fabric leaving a 1cm (½in) seam allowance within the shape using appliqué scissors. Create notches in the seam allowance to allow the fabric to sit flat and reduce fabric bulk when turned under. When cutting notches, use a sharp pair of scissors and cut about 2–3mm (¹/₁₆–³/₁₆in) short of the drawn design shape.

3 Work an appliqué stitch with coordinating machine thread from the background fabric into the top layer of fabric at 2mm (¹/₁₆in) spacing, turning the seam allowance under as you are stitching.

4 Once you have returned to the first stitch, cast off the machine thread and take out the tacking stitches.

Creating multiple layers

For multiple layers, this process can be worked many times to reveal many different fabrics. If you do not want the appliqué stitch to show you could also work this technique with a slip stitch to create an invisible stitch in the turned-under edge.

ADDING TEXTURE AND INTEREST

Frayed edges and gathers can be used to give texture and interest. Select the fabric you wish to use and then fray the edge. Once the edge is frayed you can work a running stitch through the fabric to create pleats and gathers specifically where you want and then diagonally tack this fabric down, or you can create pleats and gathers as you go. Usually the solid and unfrayed area of the fabric is secured down behind another piece of appliqué with a herringbone stitch or a series of long and short stitches.

FRAYED EDGES AND GATHERS

Controlled pleats and gathers should be tacked in place before stitching; for a looser effect tacking is not required.

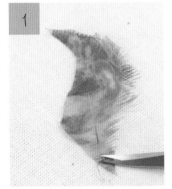

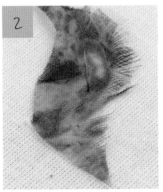

1 Cast on underneath the fabric you are applying using a knotted length of machine thread and two stitches. Cut off the knot.

2 Make stab stitches about 1mm (1/16in) long and 1cm (1/2in) apart. Work as a running stitch so that small stab stitches sit on the surface of the sheer fabric and longer stitches sit on the reverse of the fabric.

3 To create ruches and pleats, come up through the base fabric and into the sheer fabric you are applying, then take the needle down at a 45-degree angle back to your last stitch.

4 To complete the non-frayed edge, work a series of long and short stitches in one strand of machine thread. Alternatively, you could use a small herringbone stitch.

Using frayed fabrics effectively

Fiona Hart created this wonderful textured puffin piece, which is shown at full size on page 85. She used frayed edges to replicate feathers once the padding was built up for the bird's body. To control the fraying at a specific point she worked a solid stitch in the fabric and then frayed the fabric off to this point. You can use a simple machine running stitch for this or otherwise a hand backstitch. Fiona also attached this material using a herringbone stitch. A herringbone or long and short stitch can be used on fabric edges that are to be covered by subsequent appliquéd fabric.

Frayed threads are used here to represent feathers.

USING LEATHER

Kid leather comes in a wide array of colours and textures and has a certain amount of stretch. Before cutting kid leather, assess your design – if you are working leather over high relief you may need to cut the leather larger than the original flat pattern size. If in doubt, take a piece of tissue paper, fit this over your padding and draw this shape off, as this will give you a more accurate idea of the actual size required.

Always transfer your design lines onto the back of the leather – you will need to flip your design or turn your pattern piece to its reverse to achieve this. I tend to use the prick and pounce method but if you are using a template, stick the flipped template to the reverse of the leather with tape and cut around it.

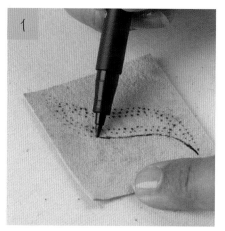

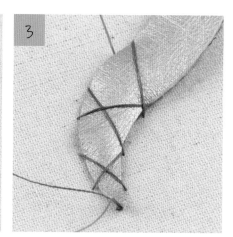

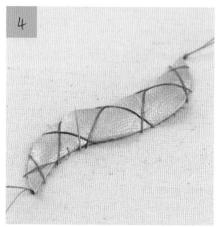
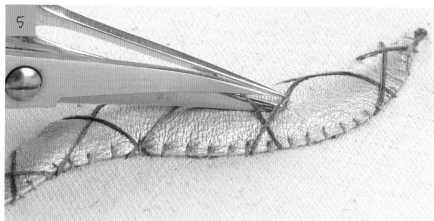

1 Pounce on the design and then use an indelible pen or HB pencil to join the dots together.

2 Cut out the leather and place it on top of the felt.

3 Work an overcast herringbone stitch over the leather to hold it in place.

4 Work appliqué stitch around the shape twice – work the first set of stitches about 4mm (³/₁₆in) apart, and then sew a second set, putting a new stitch in between each original stitch so that the stitches are about 2mm (¹/₁₆in) apart.

5 Snip the herringbone stitches with scissors, then remove the threads using a pair of tweezers.

Edging inspiration
Your leather shape could be outlined using pearl-purl (see page 90) or with cords (see page 65).

USING HEAVYWEIGHT IRON-ON INTERFACING

Heavyweight iron-on interfacings, such as pelmet Vilene, are traditionally used for making curtain pelmets but are also very useful for creating appliqué shapes that stand proud of a background. They give a different texture to a layer of felt and can also be used without a felt padded layer on top.

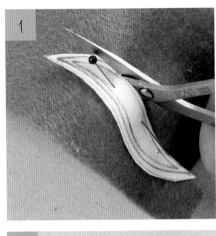
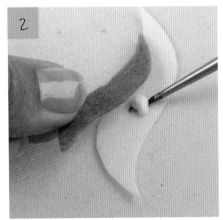
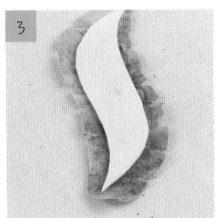
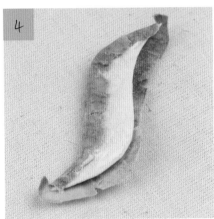
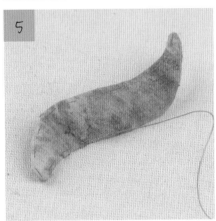

1 Pin on your design template. Cut to the felt line, which should sit 2mm (1/16in) inside the outer design line.

2 Cut the heavyweight interfacing using either a template or a pricking. Put a small dab of conservation or tacky glue onto the interfacing and stick the felt onto this.

3 Cut the fabric out so that it has 1cm (½in) allowance all the way around the interfacing. Cut small, evenly spaced notches into curves.

4 Press the fabric allowance to the back and secure with tacking stitches.

5 The interfaced shape can be stitched down using slip stitch so that the stitches don't show.

USING ADHESIVES

FUSIBLE WEB

Using an adhesive such as Bondaweb or Mistifuse is the easiest way of applying a piece of fabric to your base layer of fabric. Your fabric piece is simply ironed onto the background fabric and no tacking is required. Remember that adhesives cannot be used over padding.

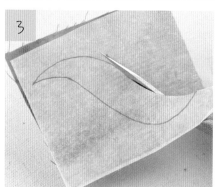

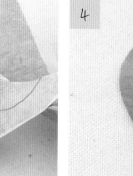

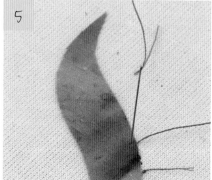

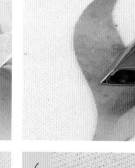

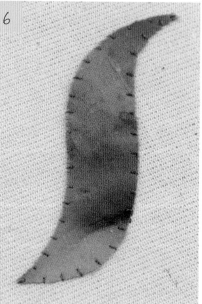

1 Turn your line design over so that you are tracing from the reverse and the design is a mirror image; alternatively, create a mirror image using a photocopier. Trace off your flipped design using an H pencil onto the iron-resistant side of a piece of fusible web.

2 Place the fusible web adhesive-side-down (rough-side-down) onto the reverse of the fabric. Fold a piece of baking paper so that it sandwiches all the elements together and then iron on top of the baking paper.

3 Remove the baking paper and let the fabric cool to room temperature. Cut the shape out on the design line.

4 Peel off the iron-resistant paper. Place the fabric adhesive-side-down on your background fabric and iron it in place.

5 Cast on one strand of machine thread in the background fabric just beside the fabric you are applying. Create two stitches and then cut off the knot.

6 Work an appliqué stitch the whole way around the shape. An appliqué stitch is always worked by coming up in the background fabric and biting into the fabric you are applying. Stitches should be roughly 2mm ($^1/_{16}$in) apart.

Machine stitching

Once fabric is adhered to the base fabric layer, why not try a machine zigzag or decorative wide stitch as an alternative to hand stitching the appliqué piece down.

Creating a mirror image

To get an accurate mirror image, flatten the reverse of the pin pricks on the pricking by gently buffering them away with sandpaper. Then pounce through the reverse of the pricking.

USING BIAS BINDING

Fusible bias binding tape is available in many colours and is often used for a technique called 'stained glass appliqué', where raw fabric edges are disguised with bias binding tape to look like leaded panes in a window (see the cockerel piece on page 104). The binding is cut on the bias so curved shapes are easily outlined. Bias binding is usually machine zigzag or machine running stitched on each side of the binding; alternative machine or hand stitches can be used.

If you are building up a stained glass appliqué you should apply the background fabrics first – usually these are bonded with an adhesive – and then you apply the bias binding on top to complete the appliqué.

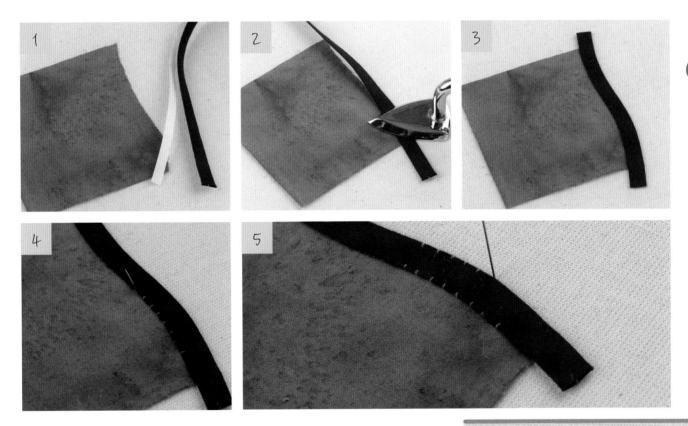

1 Appliqué stitch your base fabric down. Peel off the backing paper on the bias binding.

2 Iron the bias binding down over the top of the fabric edge, making sure the fabric edge sits to the middle of the width of the bias binding.

3 Leave the binding adhesive to cool to room temperature.

4 Cast on a machine thread (here I used a contrasting thread so that the stitches are clearly visible) and create an appliqué stitch that comes up in the base layer and goes down into the binding strip.

5 Repeat an appliqué stitch on the opposite side of the binding.

Alternative method
Alternatively, the bias binding can be machined along each edge once it has been ironed down.

USING FREEZER PAPER

Freezer paper is useful for appliqué as it has a shiny plastic side that is fusible to fabrics when ironed. Once you have attached your shape to your fabric by ironing, the freezer paper can be removed by cutting through the reverse of the fabric.

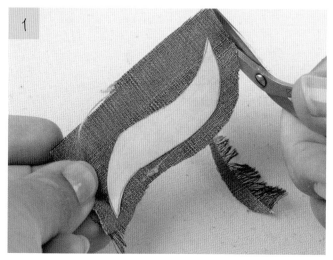

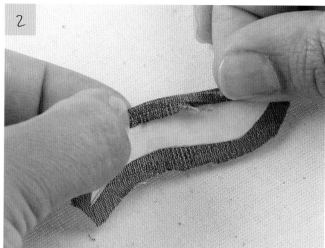

1 Cut out your design from freezer paper, and iron the shiny side to the back of your fabric. Cut a 5mm (¼in) allowance the whole way round.

2 Fold the allowance over and then press this again with an iron or with your fingers.

3 Thread up one strand of machine thread into a small embroidery needle. Knot the tail and then cast on with two stitches right underneath the edge of your shape, then cut off the knot so you are ready to begin the stitch. Create a turned edge with a slip stitch. A slip stitch is made by coming up in the background fabric and then scooping back through 1mm (¹/₁₆in) of the fold of the fabric you are applying, then taking the needle back down into the background fabric and repeating this process (see also pages 50–51).

4 Once you have completed about three to five stitches, give the thread a gentle tug and the stitches will disappear. The aim is to create an invisible stitch.

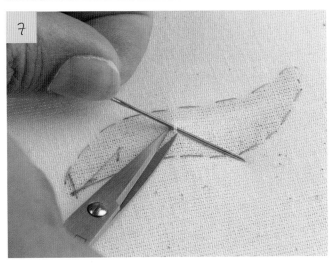

5 Continue the slip stitch up to the point of the shape and then sweep the fabric under the freezer paper with a pair of tweezers to create a sharp point in the fabric. Bring the needle up through the fabric you are applying at the very tip of the shape.

6 Continue slip stitch until you return to your starting stitch. To cast off this stitch you can either cast off by pushing the fabric to one side and slipping a few stitches behind the shape you are applying or continue round with two more slip stitches in between those you initially worked and cut the thread to cast off.

7 Turn the frame over so that you can see the backing fabric. Lift some of the threads of the calico (muslin) using a tapestry needle and snip these fibres.

8 Cut a slit into the calico (muslin) and then carefully pull the freezer paper out through the gap using a pair of fine tweezers. Make the slit as small as possible to avoid weakening the base fabric.

EDGING

Most of the edging stitches I have demonstrated use two threads of stranded embroidery cotton and a size 9 embroidery needle, but you can use a different number of threads, and of differing weights, depending on the effect you wish to achieve. If you are unsure, try them out first.

STRANDING OUT

When working embroidered edges or creating embroidery stitches with more than one strand of embroidery thread, it is important that you strand the threads out one at a time and then place them back together, so that the threads lie flat together and are not twisted up. To strand out embroidery threads, hold them at the top of the thread and then pull one out at a time. Lay them together on a table so they are grouped back up ready for use. The number of threads you use will be dependent on the effect you want to achieve, but generally I use between one and three strands for embroidery stitches and edging appliqué.

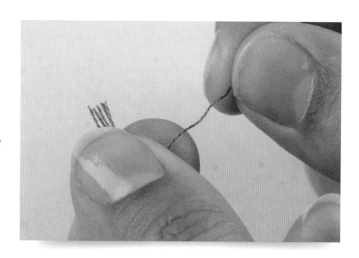

BUTTONHOLE STITCH EDGING

Buttonhole edging, if worked tightly, can be worked over the initial appliqué stitch and will successfully hide it. If you want to work an open buttonhole stitch, it is wise not to do the initial appliqué stitch into the fabric – instead, secure the fabric initially with fusible web.

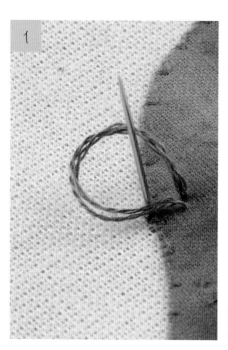

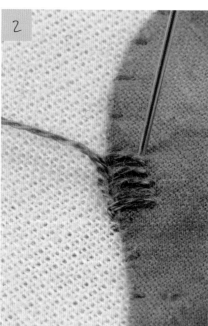

1 Strand out two strands of embroidery thread and then pair them back up. Thread them into the needle and knot the end. Cast on at the edge of the applied fabric and come up in the fabric with the thread. Take the needle down directly next to where the thread came up, leaving a slack loop of thread on the fabric surface. Bring up the needle on the edge of the applied fabric and catch the loop with your needle.

2 Continue to take the needle down into the fabric and catch the loop on the edge of the fabric to create a buttonhole edge.

SATIN STITCH EDGING

This stitch produces a crisp edge and a smooth finish. The stitch can be worked with a split stitch edge first if you require a more raised finish (see page 119).

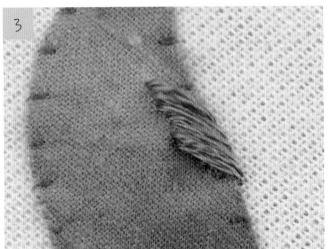

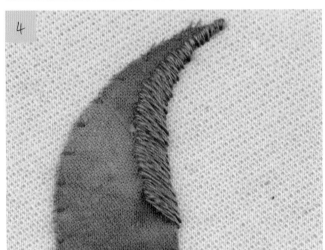

1 Cast on with two stitches and then cut off the knot. Bring up your needle at the edge of the appliquéd piece of fabric and take your needle down into the fabric at a 45-degree angle.

2 Bring up the needle in the fabric next to where you have just taken it through; take it back down into the background fabric, following the 45-degree angle.

3 Continue working the satin stitch coming up in the fabric and returning the needle back into the calico (muslin) background.

4 As you reach the top of the shape your stitches should curve around naturally to echo it. Once you reach the tip, cast off your stitches. Return to your starting point and work as before down towards the bottom of the shape.

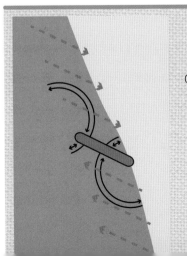

Working at an angle
Once you have set your angle with your first stitch you should always come up with your needle at the wider angle and take your needle down at the smaller angle.

COUCHED EDGING

Couched edges are used to neaten off and conceal the initial appliqué stitches that secure the fabric down. When deciding how many threads to use for your core thread, take a look at the size of the appliqué stitch you are concealing and this will guide you. Always strand out your threads and place them back together so they are not twisted up on each other (see page 60).

1 Cast on the thread beside the applied fabric with a knot and two stitches and then cut off the thread.

2 Come up with your needle at the edge of the fabric and then take the needle down over the core threads.

3 Work evenly sized, evenly tensioned stitches that follow the shape of the fabric.

FINISHING A COUCHED EDGE GRADUALLY

The neatest way to end a point on a corner is to take the threads down to the reverse of the frame (known as plunging) gradually so that you get a smooth finish to the stitch. Threads are taken through to the reverse with a large chenille or large-eyed embroidery needle. Always take the threads down gradually through different areas of the base fabric.

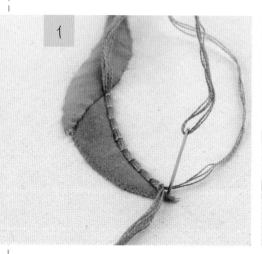 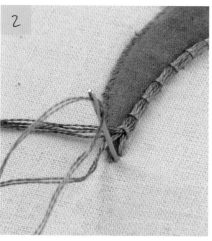 

1 Thread up the three core threads that sit closest to the surface of the base fabric and take them down next to the last couching stitch into the base fabric.

2 Take down the next two or three core threads nearest to the base fabric's surface, this time using a different hole, nearer to the point of the shape. Continue until you have one core thread left.

3 Take the final top core thread down to the reverse of the fabric at the very point of the shape.

4 Put a final couching stitch at the same spaced interval at the tip of the shape to finish it off. Finally, cast the plunged core threads off on the reverse with a curved needle and machine thread (see page 64 for further information).

63

PLUNGING CORE THREADS USING THE LASSO METHOD

Where you do not want a graduated end at a sharp point you can take the core threads down in one go, provided your core threads are not too thick. When using a large quantity of core threads, plunge them through the base fabric in close but different holes.

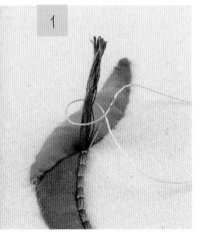

1 Create a lasso on your size 9 embroidery needle or similar: pass a length of buttonhole thread through the eye of the needle and then return the thread back through the other side of the eye to create a loop. Put the core threads into the lasso loop.

2 Pull the lasso tight to catch the ends of the core threads.

3 Pull the needle down gradually, taking the lasso and the threads with it.

4 Cast the plunged core threads off on the reverse with a curved needle and machine thread (see page 64 for further information).

Using a chenille needle to plunge core threads
Alternatively, open up the fabric by taking down an unthreaded chenille needle. Catch the core threads in the eye of a chenille needle and pull the threads through to the reverse of the fabric. Cast them off with a curved needle (see page 64 for further information).

COUCHING A CORNER QUICKLY

This method does not involve plunging, which makes it faster, but the result is that you will not create as sharp a point to your shape.

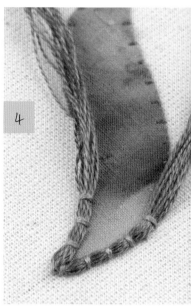

1 Cast on the thread beside the applied fabric with a knot and two stitches, then cut off the knot. Couch over the core thread at regular intervals, making sure your stitches are all the same tension.

2 When you reach a corner, stitch over the core threads right at the tip, then create a locking stitch by making a small stitch in the background fabric just in front of the corner of fabric.

3 Bring up the needle on the edge of the background calico (muslin) and create the next stitch along, couching over the core threads as before.

4 Continue working this couching stitch over the core thread. Once you reach the top of the shape you will need to plunge both sets of core threads to the reverse.

CASTING OFF PLUNGED THREADS

All plunged threads should be cast off on the reverse of the fabric using a curved needle and a double strand of machine thread. Turn your frame over to the reverse and if you are working in a ring frame, lay it on a table so it is supported.

Holding a curved needle
When using a curved needle, hold it at the base of the needle rather than the eye or the tip, as you will have more control of it at this flatter point.

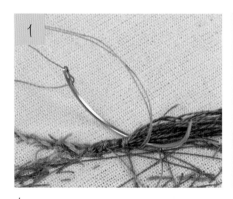

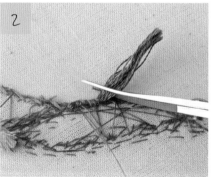

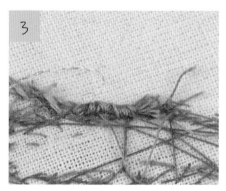

1 Cast on the thread with a knot at the plunged point of the core threads. Work four overcast stitches that secure it to the calico (muslin), working towards the tail end.

2 Work a further four overcast stitches back towards the plunged point and then cut off the tails.

3 Cut off the machine thread.

64

CORDED EDGING

Corded edges look beautiful and can give a lovely finish. In this demonstration I have couched a cord over a turned edge, but you can also do this on an appliqué edge to conceal the stitches. (See pages 68–69 for how to make a cord.)

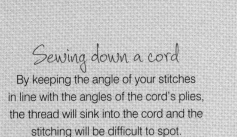

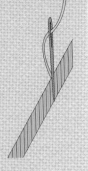

Sewing down a cord

By keeping the angle of your stitches in line with the angles of the cord's plies, the thread will sink into the cord and the stitching will be difficult to spot.

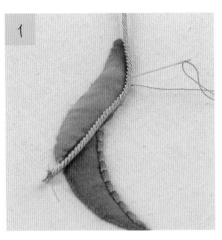

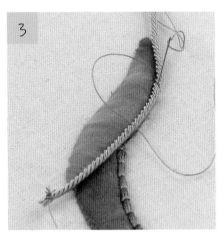

1 Lay down the cord around the edge of the applied fabric to conceal the fabric join with the background fabric. Thread up one strand of machine thread in a small embroidery needle. Start the stitch with two casting on stitches on the underside of the cord, cut the waste knot off and then make a long diagonal stitch from the outer edge of the applied fabric into the cord, taking the needle down into the far side of the cord.

2 Come up for the next long diagonal stitch in the applied fabric.

3 Take the needle down into the cord on the furthest twist from the applied fabric. Continue working diagonally opposite stitches all the way along the cord.

TWISTING UP A CORD AROUND A CORNER

There are two ways of applying cord around a corner of fabric: either twist up the cord a little more and work it around the applied fabric edge, or take the cords down to the reverse of the fabric and cast them off (see page 66).

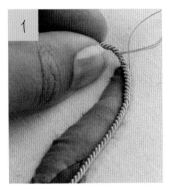

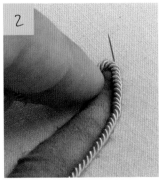

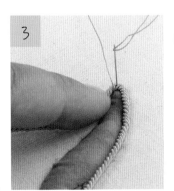

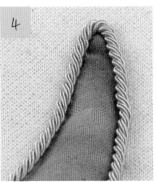

1 Once you reach close to the tip or corner of the applied fabric, begin twisting up the cord by rotating it in your fingers.

2 Manipulate it so that it follows the shape of the fabric. Continue the diagonal alternation angle stitch (shown above) around the corner.

3 The stitches should follow the twists of the cord – they should be more frequent and at a smaller angle to match the way the twists fall.

4 Once working back from the corner, let the cord untwist to its usual tension and continue to work the alternating long diagonal stitches.

PLUNGING CORDS TO ACHIEVE A SHARP-POINTED CORNER

To complete a cord with a sharp corner, the most effective way of doing so is to plunge the cords through to the reverse of the base fabric and cast them off. If you are plunging a small cord it may be possible to plunge the cord to the reverse using a stiletto or large chenille needle. Larger cords should be separated into their individual cores and taken through to the reverse through individual holes to prevent stress and tears across the fabric's surface.

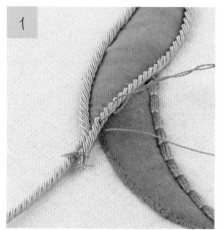

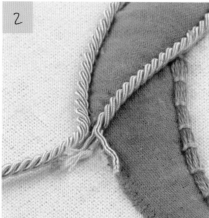

1 Make a final stitch near to the area where the cord is going to be plunged but not right at the point as the stitch is liable to break when plunging.

2 Separate the plies of the cord.

3 Take the ply that is sitting closest to the base fabric down through the fabric using a buttonhole thread lasso (see tip box right and finishing a couched thread, page 63).

4 The first ply of cord has now been plunged.

5 With the first ply taken through to the reverse, the next ply closest to the base fabric should be taken down using a lasso in the same way. Use a different hole, close to the first.

6 Take down the final ply – it should be plunged in a position so that it looks like the cord continues on down through the fabric. Cast off on the reverse using a curved needle and a double machine thread (see page 64).

7 Sew a few long diagonal stitches into the end of the cord to secure the ends down.

66

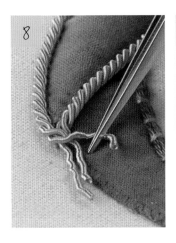  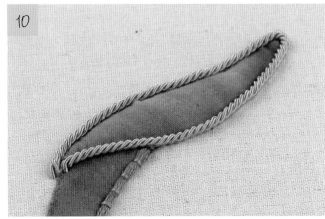

8 With the first end of the cord plunged, the second must be carefully manipulated to achieve a sharp point. You are aiming to take the second set of cords down below the first, to overlap them slightly and create a chevroned finish. As before, start with the ply closest to the fabric first, then plunge all subsequent plies, taking the top ply down last. Cast off the threads on the back of the fabric.

9 Put some long diagonal stitches into the end of the cord to secure it.

10 The completed corner should look neat – this technique creates a much sharper point than you would achieve by twisting up the cord at the corner.

Making a lasso

To make a lasso, take a 20cm (8in) length of buttonhole thread and pass one end through the eye of a needle and then take the other end of the thread back through the opposite side. Position this loop around your threads to be plunged, tighten it, then pull the needle through to the back of the fabric, dragging the cord with it.

CASTING OFF CORD ENDS

Fine cords need to be bound prior to plunging them to the reverse of the fabric. This is done by making several stitches into the cord's tail using a sharp small needle and two strands of machine thread. Thicker cords are split so that each ply of the cord is taken down through the base fabric individually.

Cast off the cord ends using two strands of machine thread looped through the eye of a small curved needle. Make several stitches starting directly at the plunge, working towards the core tails and then back towards the plunge.

After completing a cord plunge I like to cast off on the reverse immediately, before completing the next cord plunge. I find that being systematic in this way keeps my work much tidier.

MAKING CORDS

You can purchase ready-made cords but it is a lot more fun to make your own, and doing so means that you can tailor your colours to your own project. Cords can be made as two-ply, three-ply or four-ply, and differing quantities of threads can be used to give different weights to each of the cords. Cord-making can be done alone but it is a lot easier to ask a friend to help you. For this cord I am going to make a three-ply cord using six strands of thread in each ply.

68

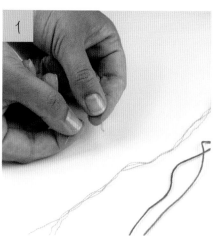

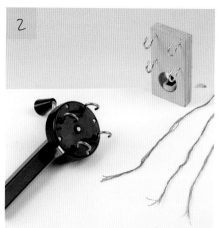

1 Always strand out individual threads (see page 60) – do not use them directly from the skein as they are twisted and will not make a smooth cord. Create three stranded sets of threads in the colour and length of your choice.

2 Attach the hooks to the edge of a table using a clamp.

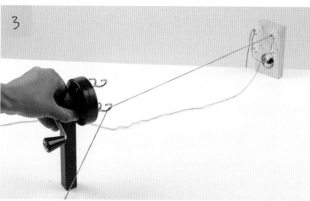

3 Knot each set of threads to a hook, then knot them to a hook on the cord winder, making sure that all the threads are of the same length and tension.

4 Keeping the metal button on the top of the cord winder held in, rotate the handle. This spins each of your sets of threads individually.

5 Once the thread plies start to crinkle up on themselves, stop rotating the handle and release the metal button.

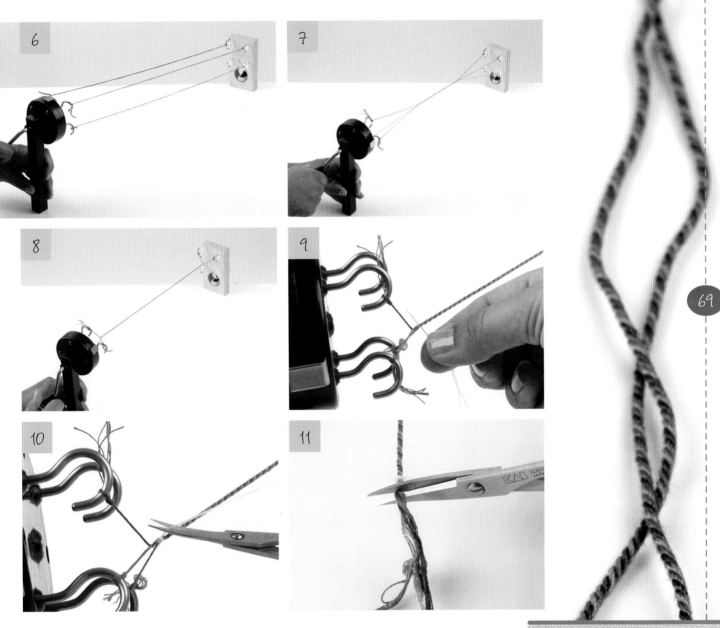

6 With your thread groups twisted, turn the handle again, this time without pressing in the button so that all the plies rotate together.

7 You will see the individual plies begin to twist together. Continue to turn the handle until the twists are continuous from the cord winder to the hooks.

8 Keep the cord at a tight tension.

9 Ask someone to hold the cord winder for you, or support it carefully, so that you can keep the tension on it. Cast off the cord with a double machine thread by running a sharp needle through the cord several times to create securing stitches. You will require additional stitches if your cord is thick.

10 Cut off the tail of machine thread.

11 Cut off the ends of the cord at both ends, so that they are tidy and can be easily plunged.

Alternative method

It is also possible to make a cord using a drill with a cord-making attachment. Cords can also be made using two pencils and a volunteer or alternatively, a volunteer at one end and a hook at the other to replace the volunteer.

SILK SHADING

Silk shading, also known as painting with a needle, is a stunning technique that can replicate shade and dimensions and is very useful for appliqué. I use this technique to shade areas in solid stitch and to edge areas of appliqué to cover raw fabric edges. Sometimes, I will work areas off the main frame in the form of slips and then apply them to the main frame.

CREATING SILK SHADING

The technique of silk shading comprises two stitches: split stitch and long and short stitch. Although called long and short stitch, it is really a technique consisting of long and longer stitches. When working a design in long and short stitch, the background areas are worked prior to the foreground.

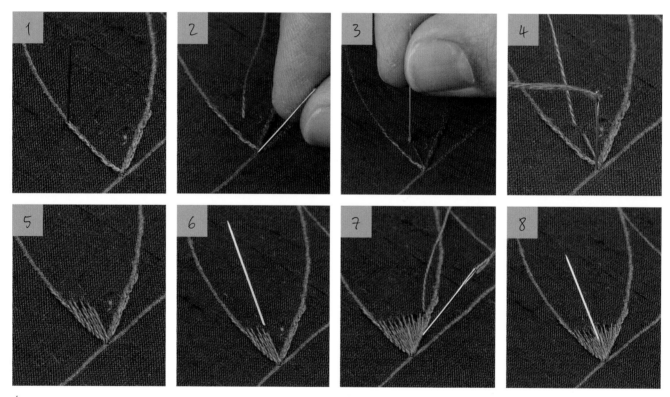

1 Create a split stitch edge around the area you are going to work (see page 117).

2 Bring up the needle in the centre of the area you are going to work and take the stitch down over the split-stitch edge.

3 Bring up the needle just beyond the first stitch.

4 Take the needle back down over the split stitch edge, as you did in step 2.

5 Work a series of long and shorter stitches from the middle out towards the left-hand edge.

6 Bring up the needle in the middle of the shape.

7 Work a series of long and shorter stitches from the middle out towards the right-hand edge. Cast off the threads and thread up with a darker colour.

8 For all subsequent rows of long and short stitch you should split the stitches made in the previous row. Bring up the needle a third of the way down a stitch in the previous row.

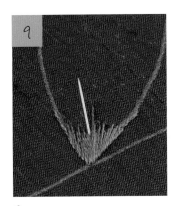

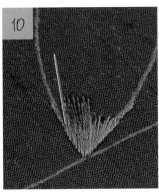

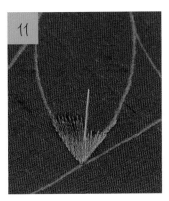

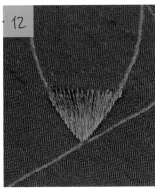

9 Create the first stitch. Bring up the needle in the stitch next to the first one you split – make sure you split each stitch at different points so that you do not get a solid line of stitch showing, and so the stitches are blended across each row.

10 When you reach the end of a row and run out of stitches to pierce through (usually where a shape widens) you can add a few additional stitches over the edge of your split stitch to form a complete row of long and short stitches.

11 Return to the middle of the row and continue to split through the first row of long and short stitches from the middle to the right-hand edge.

12 Once you have split all the threads in the first row and have worked to the outer edge to completely fill the shape you can begin a third row of long and short, if desired. All further rows are worked in the same way – splitting the threads in the row before.

71

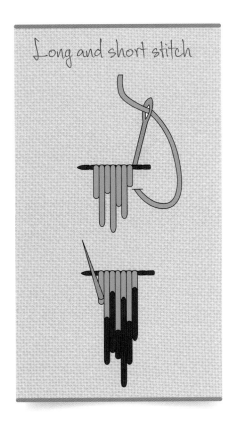

Long and short stitch

Cosmos
15 x 20cm (6 x 8in)
Kate Cross

Silk shaded petals combined with goldwork techniques.

Fern

9 x 9cm (3½ x 3½in)

This initial project includes many of the differing edges and stitches I have demonstrated so far and can be worked in a 20cm (8in) embroidery ring frame. This project is a good starting point for putting all of the techniques together into a composition and will build on your technical appliqué skills. All the padded areas are on the right-hand side of the design and the other two layers on the left-hand side require no padding.

Going on or off grain

When working appliqué correctly, the grain of all the fabrics should match, which is known as being 'on the grain'; this way all the fabrics sit together at the correct tension and the stretch quantities of the fabric are similar. For the organza leaf (see step 9, page 76) I have chosen to have the grain of the fabric at a diagonal to the background fabric for artistic quality. Silk and metal organza have very little stretch so this is an ideal fabric to position off grain.

YOU WILL NEED

TOOLS

Design (see page 74)

Pricker

Chalk or cuttlefish pounce

Watercolour paint in ochre colour

A fine size 000 paintbrush

Tracing paper

HB propelling pencil

Photocopier (optional)

Tissue paper

20cm (8in) ring frame

Pins: preferably silk or appliqué pins

Sharp needles: chenille for plunging and a small embroidery needle

Fine point tweezers

Mellor

Iron-on adhesive

Freezer paper

Sharp embroidery scissors

Appliqué scissors

A cord winder (optional)

FABRICS

Calico (muslin): 25 x 25cm (10 x 10in)

Purple silk: 25 x 25cm (10 x 10in)

Three golden shades of silk: 10 x 10cm (4 x 4in) of each

Purple velvet: 10 x 10cm (4 x 4in)

Silk organza: 5 x 5cm (2 x 2in)

Carpet felt or 100% wool extra thick felt: 7 x 4cm (2¾ x 1½in)

Felt: 15 x 15cm (6 x 6in)

THREADS

Machine threads in coordinating colours: white, purple, gold

Embroidery stranded cottons in coordinating colours: purple, pink, golden-brown, red

Ready-made cord, or the component embroidery cottons to make a cord

DESIGN TEMPLATE

Trace this basic design layout at full size and take photocopies of the design areas so that you can create templates. Be flexible in your approach, and adapt my design to make it your own. I have labelled this image to indicate which techniques have been used; follow the order of work given to complete the project. Change up the colours, fabrics and techniques to suit your own taste, and don't forget that if you don't want to make your own cord from scratch, you can easily purchase it ready-made.

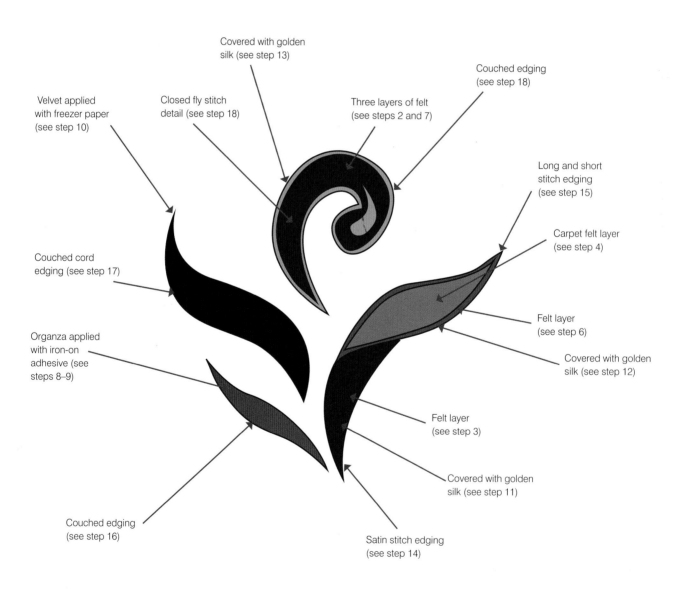

Covered with golden silk (see step 13)

Couched edging (see step 18)

Velvet applied with freezer paper (see step 10)

Closed fly stitch detail (see step 18)

Three layers of felt (see steps 2 and 7)

Long and short stitch edging (see step 15)

Carpet felt layer (see step 4)

Couched cord edging (see step 17)

Felt layer (see step 6)

Organza applied with iron-on adhesive (see steps 8–9)

Covered with golden silk (see step 12)

Felt layer (see step 3)

Covered with golden silk (see step 11)

Couched edging (see step 16)

Satin stitch edging (see step 14)

ORDER OF WORK

1 Sew the silk onto a backing fabric of calico (muslin) in a slate frame (see pages 24–29). The calico (muslin) will give the silk extra support for the weight of the padding. Transfer the design onto the silk using the prick and pounce method. Go over the lines with paint, then brush away the pounce.

2 The next stage is padding. The right-hand leaf with the turnover is composed of one layer of felt in the lower half of the leaf. Layers of carpet felt and felt make up the leaf's turnover. The curled fern frond is made up of three layers of felt, as indicated by the template. Mark out all of these padded shapes using the prick and pounce method and cut out.

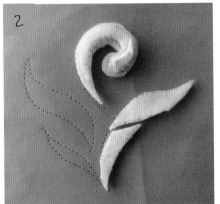

3 Pin the lower half of the right-hand leaf in place, so that the felt sits directly against the design lines. Sew down the felt using appliqué stitch; sew once around, spacing the stitches 4mm (³/₁₆in) apart, then sew round a second time, applying extra stitches between these initial stitches (see pages 48–49).

4 Chamfer the edges of your carpet felt shape. Pin it in place, then secure it down by working a herringbone stitch from one end to the other, using a doubled machine thread.

5 Sew long and short stitch around the edge of the carpet felt to neaten it and ensure graduated edges. Remove the herringbone tacking stitches (not shown).

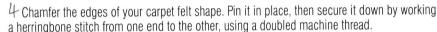

6 Place your felt layer on top of the carpet felt to ensure that it is the correct size, then work an appliqué stitch around the edges to secure it.

7 The fern frond is made up of three layers of felt for a high relief. Start with the smallest piece and position it with a pin. Appliqué stitch once round the shape. It is not necessary to do this twice as it will be covered, and only the final layer of felt requires the perfectly smooth edges achieved with closer stitches. Apply the second layer in the same way as the first. Pin the third and final layer in place. Sew down the felt using appliqué stitch; sew around the shape twice to create a neat, even finish.

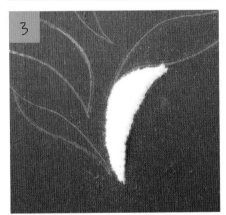

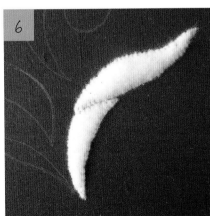

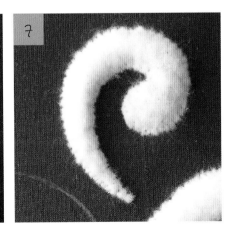

8 Iron some fusible web adhesive to the back of a piece of gold-coloured silk. Use your template to draw out a reversed version of the lower left-hand leaf shape onto the back of the adhesive. Cut out the fabric shape along the design line.

9 Peel off the adhesive backing and iron this shape to the background fabric on a medium heat. Appliqué stitch using a machine thread around the applied organza to secure the fabric entirely (not shown).

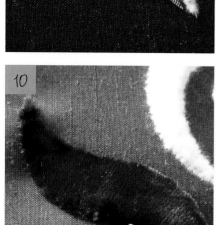

10 The velvet leaf is applied using the freezer paper method (see pages 58–59). Draw the reversed shape onto freezer paper, cut this out and iron onto the back of a piece of velvet, using a medium heat. Cut out the velvet shape, leaving a 5mm (¼in) allowance all the way around. Cut notches into this excess fabric so that it turns under and sits neatly around the curves of the freezer paper. Position the velvet on the fabric – pinning or tacking with herringbone stitch if need be – tucking all the edges under. Secure the velvet in place using a turned edge (see pages 50–51) using a single strand of coordinating machine thread.

11 Use your template to cut out the fabric shapes needed to cover the top and bottom of the right-hand leaf. Start with the bottom section of the right-hand leaf, as this sits the flattest in the design. Use a herringbone stitch to secure the fabric in place. Use an appliqué stitch to secure the raw edges of the fabric in place (see pages 48–49). Remove the tacking stitches.

12 Repeat step 11 to cover the top section of the right-hand leaf.

13 Use your template to cut out the fabric shape needed to cover the fern frond. Tack it in place with a herringbone stitch over the padding, to check that it fits. Use an appliqué stitch to secure the raw edges of the fabric in place.

14 Create the edging on the bottom half of the right-hand leaf shape – I worked this leaf first as it is the lowest of the padded areas. Starting midway up the right-hand edge, work a satin stitch outwards (see page 119). I didn't put any split stitch down first as I wanted the inside of the leaf to be free and gradual, rather than a solid block. I would advise against putting a split stitch on the inside edge on top of the fabric as the appliqué stitch may work loose as you pull through the felt. The other, outer edge can be split stitched if it helps you work a neater satin stitch.

15 To create the edging for the turnover, work long and short stitch in two strands of embroidery cotton, so that it fills in densely. Along the edges of the shape I worked two or three stitches, but at the ends of the shape I created solid rows. I worked with two different gold shades of thread but you could adapt this according to the effect you require.

16 To create the couched edging on the organza leaf, sew down seven stranded-out core embroidery threads using one thread to couch them down. I used two sets of core threads – one on each side of the shape – so that they could be plunged at both ends to form a sharp point at each tip.

17 If you want to make your own cord, do so according to the instructions on pages 68–69, otherwise use ready-made cord; you will need a 20cm (8in) length. Starting at the top tip of the velvet leaf, secure the cord in place using diagonal stitches (see page 65).

18 Remove the tacking threads from the fern frond. Sew a closed fly stitch up the length of the frond, working from the top to the bottom. To complete, couch down golden-brown stranded embroidery threads around the edge to conceal the raw edge. Start and finish at the pointed tip of the shape, plunging the threads down to the back of the frame to complete.

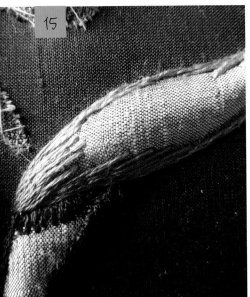

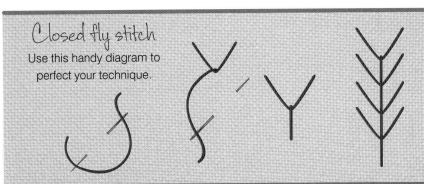

Closed fly stitch
Use this handy diagram to perfect your technique.

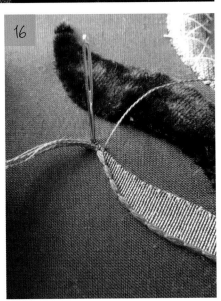

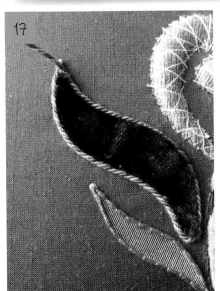

IN DETAIL

Here you can see a combination of edges in detail on the right-hand side: the finished satin stitch edge tapers gently up the edge of the lower leaf.

Long and short stitch worked over carpet felt padding. The long and short stitch was worked in rows using different tones for a shaded dimensional effect to the leaf's turnover. Long and short stitch can be worked against raw edges to cover any frayed fabric edges. When working solid stitches like this, keep your stitch tension consistent and not too tight so that the fabric stays smooth and you don't distort the felt underneath the fabric.

Silk organza placed off the grain for effect. When working with an open fabric such as organza, make sure your initial appliqué stitches, which hold the fabric down, vary a little in size as the piece of organza can pull away from the background fabric if your stitches are on the same grain line throughout the fabric.

The frond of the fern is created over felt padding and the fabric is secured down with a small appliqué stitch. This appliqué stitch is subsequently covered using a couched edge. When deciding the thickness of the couching core, look at all your appliqué stitches and use the largest stitch as a guide to work out how many threads to use for your core as these stitches should be covered using this couching edge.

Two Birds

32 x 41cm (12¾ x 16in)

Constance Howard, courtesy of the Embroiderers' Guild

A rayon with wool twill fabric panel in appliqué and surface embroidery, using various stitches; made in England in 1950.

The Great Grey Heron
42 x 34cm (16½ x 13½in)
Linda Kilgore

This piece is worked on 36-count linen and was hand-painted before the embroidery was worked.

Parrot on a Branch with Berries

41 x 37cm (16 x 14½in)

Michael Bingham

The inspiration for this design comes from a 17th-century *pietra dura* panel in a Florentine cabinet. The design gave the freedom to use a wonderful colourful palette.

A Floral Arrangement

55 x 47cm (21²/₃ x 18½in)

Anne Rowan

An appliqué piece with some stumpwork wired elements, completed for the Royal School of Needlework Diploma, inspired by a painting by Mary Elizabeth Duffield (1819–1914) entitled *Roses and Lilies*.

Fishing Spiderman

44 x 49cm (17½ x 19½in)

Mimi Chan

Layers of carpet felt and stuffing are used to give depth to the image and create a three-dimensional effect. Layers of sheer and cotton fabrics have been adhered to create the waves.

Flowers in a Vase
30 x 38cm (12 x 15in)
Yukari Suai

This piece was designed based on paintings by the artist Paul Augustin Aizpiri. Several fabric manipulation techniques were used to create a three-dimensional look.

Puffin
31 x 26cm (12 x 10¼in)
Fiona Hart

The puffin was worked on blue silk to indicate a background of sea and sky. Kid leather was used for the feet and sand eels, and dyed cotton for the beak, with a variety of edging techniques including trailing for the beak and the use of pearl-purl around the feet.

RIBBONWORK

Ribbonwork is a good supplementary technique to appliqué and can be combined easily with other techniques, such as goldwork, to create fantastic results. You can work ribbonwork with synthetic ribbon but it works best with silk, as silk is much more pliable than synthetic. Ribbons come in a range of widths, but I generally use 2mm ($\frac{1}{16}$in) to 7mm ($\frac{1}{4}$in) sizes. There are lots of different stitches that can be used for ribbonwork but many are based around a couple of basic stitches.

LOOPED FLOWER

Creating loops on the surface of the fabric is very simple but decorative. It can be combined with goldwork for a more elaborate look (see pages 88–89).

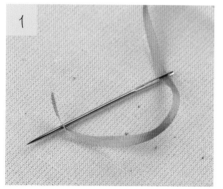

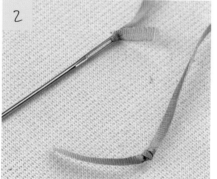

1 Thread a chenille needle with your ribbon, then place the point of the needle into the end of the ribbon, about 1cm ($\frac{1}{2}$in) from the end.

2 Pull the needle through the tail end to secure the ribbon to the needle. Tie a knot in the other end of the ribbon.

3 Bring up the needle, then take it back down as close as you can next to your ribbon.

4 Do not pull the ribbon right the way through; instead leave a slack loop on the fabric surface.

5 Repeat steps 3 and 4 to create a collection of loops on the fabric surface – bring the needle up close to the previous loop so that the loops sit close together.

RIBBON STITCH FLOWER

Ribbon stitch is used frequently in ribbonwork for leaves and flowers and is a simple but effective stitch.

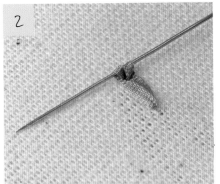

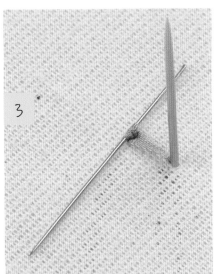

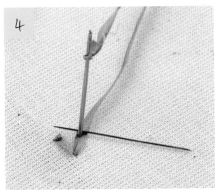

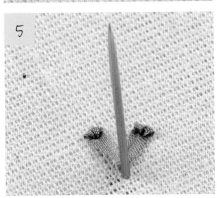

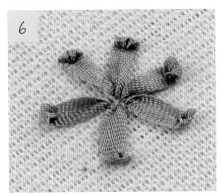

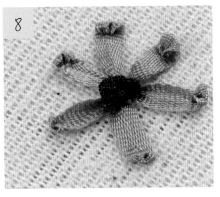

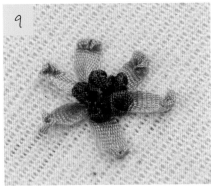

1 Secure the ribbon to the needle (see step 1, opposite) and tie a knot in the tail of the ribbon. Come up with the ribbon. Take the chenille needle back down into the ribbon but, before pulling it through, place either a fine needle or pin just above this point.

2 Pull the needle through to the reverse of the fabric.

3 Come up at the starting point again to make another stitch.

4 Again, take the chenille needle back down into the ribbon. Remove the fine needle or pin out of the first stitch and place it above the chenille needle at the second stitch. Then take the chenille needle down to the reverse.

5 Come up at the starting point again to make another stitch.

6 Continue to work this stitch to create a six-petalled flower.

7 To create a French knot centre, secure the contrasting ribbon to the needle and knot the end. Bring up the needle in the centre of the petals and make a loop around the needle towards the sharp point. Take the needle down next to where you brought it up.

8 The completed French knot.

9 Work a mass of French knots in the centre of the petals (see page 122).

USING METAL THREADS

Metal threads can be used to add glamour or sheen to a project. Here are a few ways to use them in combination with appliqué – for example, how I used them in my appliqué and goldwork necklaces (see page 90).

(see page 90)

Always use the right tools for the technique. A mellor is a really handy tool that is used to ease metal 'purls' into position and decrease the chance of fracturing and denting them with a sharp needle.

Using the right tools
Always use the right tools for the technique. A mellor is a really handy tool that is used to ease metal 'purls' into position and decrease the chance of fracturing and denting them with a sharp needle.

SEWING DOWN A PURL

There are many different colours and sizes of purl available from specialist goldwork embroidery suppliers, and they can be cut to different lengths and sewn on to fabrics in the same way as bugle beads. Purls are always sewn down using waxed doubled machine thread.

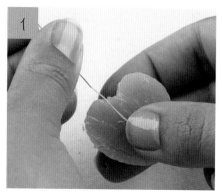

1 Thread up a double strand of machine thread through a small embroidery needle and tie a knot at the tail of the thread. Run the thread through a piece of beeswax until the thread 'squeaks'.

2 Cut the purl using serrated goldwork scissors and then cast on with two small stitches – the purl will sit on top of these and hide them. Bring up the needle and place the purl onto it; slide the purl down to the fabric's surface.

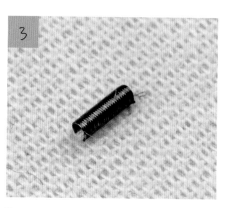

3 Take the needle back down at the end of the purl and ease it down gently using a mellor.

CREATING A PURL FLOWER CENTRE

This is a great technique for adding a decorative goldwork centre to a ribbonwork flower.

1 To create a ribbonwork flower, see pages 86–87. Cast on with a waxed doubled length of thread in the centre of the flower. Cut five identical lengths of purl.

see pages 86–87.

88

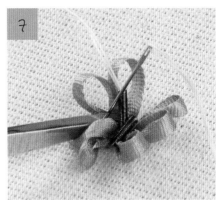

2 Place a length of purl onto the needle and slide it down to the end of the thread.

3 Take the needle back down into the centre of the flower, creating a stitch that is slightly shorter than the length of the purl, so that the purl will stand proud.

4 Ease the purl down using a mellor tool.

5 Now the first purl is secure.

6 Use the mellor to ease the first purl to the right slightly, bringing up the needle at the centre of the left-hand side. Thread on another purl.

7 Take the needle down again, directly to the left of the first purl, again making the stitch slightly shorter than the purl, and ease the purl down with the mellor.

8 Continue to work purls in the same way until you get back to the beginning. Push aside the first purl with your mellor and take the needle down.

9 Cut two purls a little shorter in length, and then work these in the same way in the centre of the flower to complete it.

The completed flower.

PEARL-PURL

Pearl-purl is most commonly used for outlining and is a spring coil that is made to look like a series of pearls. This material can also be used for outlining fabric edges. When working with pearl-purl, make sure your thread is waxed.

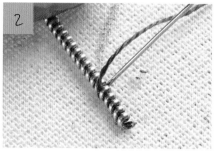

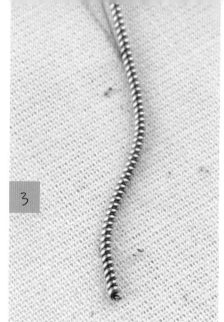

1 Cast on underneath the starting point to your pearl-purl by creating two backstitches and cutting off the waste knot. Then create the first small diagonal stitch to sit in the first groove of the metal purl.

2 Continue to make small diagonal stitches in every other groove so that the stitches run in the same direction as the pearl-purl grooves. To make sure the stitches are not visible, come up and take your needle down at an angle.

3 Once the pearl-purl is stitched down, you should cast off the thread and then cut off the pearl-purl back to the last stitch made.

Heavenly Scent necklaces
Kate Cross

These floral necklaces combine goldwork and ribbonwork with appliqué backgrounds to create striking textures. The centres of the flowers are all worked using cut and looped purls.

BRICKED COUCHING LAIDWORK METHOD

This method of couching is useful for covering an area in metal threads and could also be translated using other threads that provide different texture. I have worked this in a Japanese goldwork thread. This is an easy way of couching as it requires minimal plunging of threads through to the reverse of the fabric, as the threads are turned at corners instead.

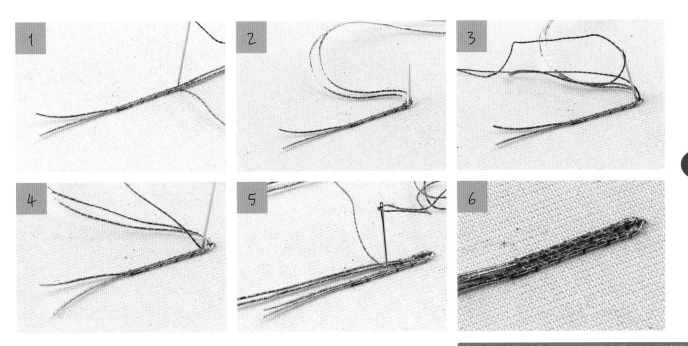

1 Leave a 5cm (2in) tail of thread for plunging, then cast on with two backstitches and cut off the waste knot. Work evenly spaced stitches over a pair of Japanese threads so that the stitch hugs the threads and secures them down to the fabric surface.

2 When turning a corner, bring up your needle in between the two threads.

3 Take your needle down on the outside edge to secure the outer Japanese thread first. Then come back up in the middle of the pair and take a stitch over the inner thread.

4 Prior to easing the Japanese threads round, make a locking stitch ahead of the threads in the fabric. This is just a small 1mm (1/16in) stitch that anchors the last corner stitch. Ease the threads round the corner and if necessary tweak them with a pair of tweezers for a sharp turn.

5 Continue onto the second row to form brick stitches. To create these stitches you should come up above the Japanese thread and take your needle down against the first row. Angle your needle slightly underneath the previous row so that both rows will sit together without gaps of fabric showing in between.

6 To form a solid area, continue working from the right to left for your third row or plunge and cast off the Japanese threads on the reverse of the fabric.

Edging inspiration
This brickwork couching could be used on raw edges of fabric that require more than one couched edge to conceal them.

BEADING

Beading and embellishing on the surface of the cotton organdy was done to prevent raw edges fraying and for additional texture. Different sized beads were combined to form intricate patterns with the rest of the layering effects.

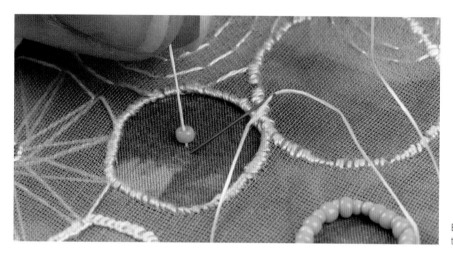

Beads are usually sewn down with nylon beading thread for strength and a fine beading needle.

CREATING A CIRCLE OF BEADS

This is the quickest and easiest method for sewing down a circle of beads.

1 Bring your needle up from the back of the fabric, and thread your chosen beads onto it. Take the string of beads around the circle and back to your starting point to check that you have the right number on the thread.

2 Take the needle back down in front of the first bead.

3 Bring up the needle in between the beads at every second or third bead in the cotton organdy and take the needle down into the indigo fabric.

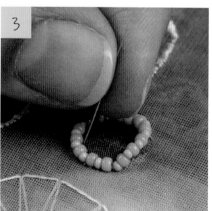

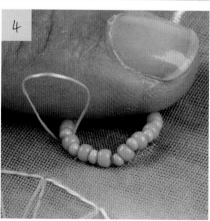

4 Continue couching between the beads until you return to the start.

CUTTING AWAY

Fabrics can be adhered together with fusible web adhesive and then embroidered in a solid stitch such as satin or fishbone to stabilise the edge. Then, fabric can be cut away to reveal underlying fabrics. Before completing this process, check the top fabric layer is of sufficient weight and colour to conceal the underlying fabric by placing your fabric underneath the top cut-away layer of fabric.

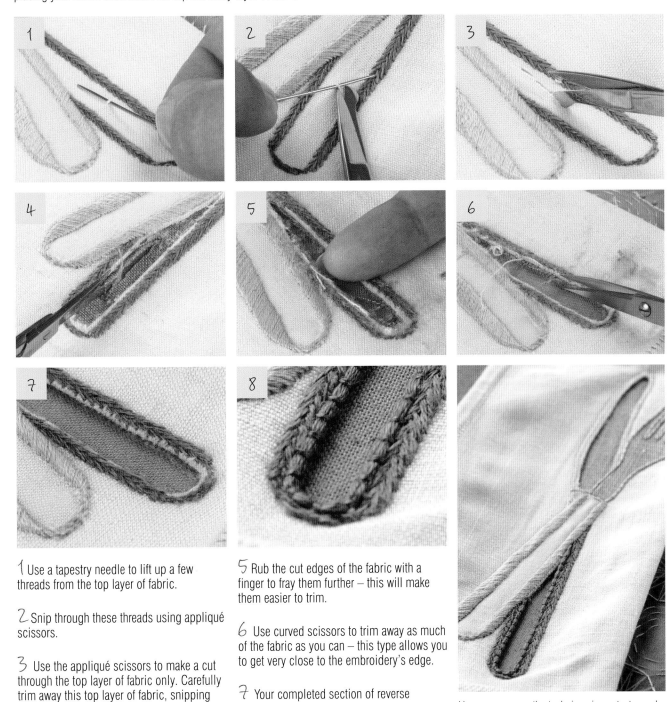

1 Use a tapestry needle to lift up a few threads from the top layer of fabric.

2 Snip through these threads using appliqué scissors.

3 Use the appliqué scissors to make a cut through the top layer of fabric only. Carefully trim away this top layer of fabric, snipping close to your stitched outline.

4 Repeat steps 1–3 until you reach the desired layer; here, the salmon-pink layer.

5 Rub the cut edges of the fabric with a finger to fray them further – this will make them easier to trim.

6 Use curved scissors to trim away as much of the fabric as you can – this type allows you to get very close to the embroidery's edge.

7 Your completed section of reverse appliqué should have a neat, crisp edge.

8 Outline the raw edge with a couching thread.

Here you can see the technique in context: used to form the handle of a knife.

Poppy

15 x 18cm (6 x 7in)

I took the photograph below at Hampton Court Palace. The textures and dimensions of this spectacular poppy were perfect to be replicated with appliqué. I hand-dyed and layered different materials and used a striking dark aubergine background to make the orange colour zing out. I dyed some of the background silks to create gradual shading rather than blocked areas of orange tone.

The project was worked on a slate frame. The velvet was applied to calico (muslin) while the frame was relatively loose; it was then tightened in order to tack the design on and then loosened again for the appliqué application. Only once all fabrics had been applied and the carpet felt was ready to be applied was the frame fully tightened.

YOU WILL NEED

TOOLS

Design (see pages 96–97)

Tracing paper

Tailors' chalk

Photocopier (optional)

Slate frame and framing up equipment: calico (muslin) backing, webbing, bracing needle, buttonhole thread

Tissue paper

Pins: preferably silk or appliqué pins

Sharp needles: chenille for plunging wires and a small embroidery needle

Sharp embroidery scissors

Appliqué scissors

Fine point tweezers

Mellor

Sewing machine

Silk dyes (optional)

FABRICS

Dark shade of velvet for the background: I used silk velvet but cotton would work too: 30 x 30cm (12 x 12in)

Orange silk dupion: 50 x 50cm (20 x 20in)

Orange cotton in several shades: 20 x 20cm (8 x 8in)

Sheer black organdy: 20 x 20cm (8 x 8in)

Carpet felt or 100% wool extra thick felt: 15 x 15cm (6 x 6in)

Green silks in three shades: 15 x 15cm (6 x 6in) each

THREADS AND BEADS

Orange machine thread

Embroidery stranded cottons in shades and colours that coordinate with the petals and the background: yellow, brown, black, green, purple

A selection of small brown beads

Fine wire for the turned petals

DESIGN TEMPLATE

Trace this basic design layout at full size. As you can see, this design contains many pieces that overlap, so to make it as clear as possible, I have also provided the individual petal shapes, right. These are labelled to correspond with the complete template below. However, be flexible in your approach, and adapt my design to make it your own. I have labelled this image to indicate which techniques have been used; follow the order of work given to complete the project.

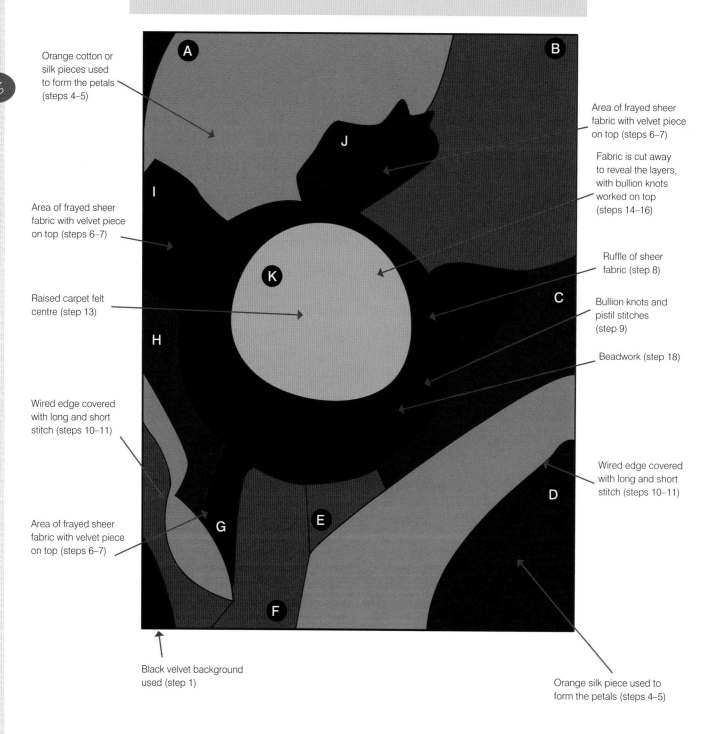

Orange cotton or silk pieces used to form the petals (steps 4–5)

Area of frayed sheer fabric with velvet piece on top (steps 6–7)

Fabric is cut away to reveal the layers, with bullion knots worked on top (steps 14–16)

Area of frayed sheer fabric with velvet piece on top (steps 6–7)

Ruffle of sheer fabric (step 8)

Raised carpet felt centre (step 13)

Bullion knots and pistil stitches (step 9)

Beadwork (step 18)

Wired edge covered with long and short stitch (steps 10–11)

Wired edge covered with long and short stitch (steps 10–11)

Area of frayed sheer fabric with velvet piece on top (steps 6–7)

Black velvet background used (step 1)

Orange silk piece used to form the petals (steps 4–5)

Use all these petal templates as a rough guide: cut them out with an additional 1cm (½in) border to ensure that they are large enough.

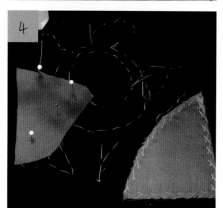

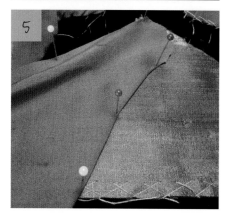

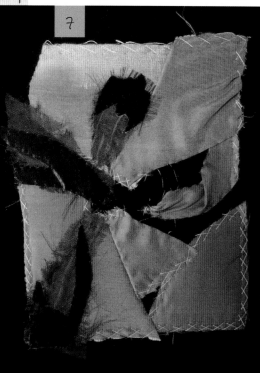

ORDER OF WORK

1 As all the stitching in this project is done by hand, start by stretching your calico (muslin) backing fabric in a slate frame, and apply your velvet background fabric (see pages 24–29, not shown).

2 Use the template to trace the key design lines onto tissue paper. Place this on your background velvet and tack it in place using parallel rows of large, diagonal stitches, worked from the middle out. Translate the design lines by working a running stitch along them using embroidery cotton; here I used yellow. Make large stitches on the surface and small stitches on the reverse. Knot all the thread tails so that when you pull away the tissue you do not pull out the tacked design lines.

3 Pull away the tissue paper, leaving your stitched design behind. If the paper gets trapped in the running stitches, ease it out with tweezers (not shown).

4 Create templates for the background petals (see page 97) and cut these from orange silk or cotton. Cut them 1cm (½in) larger than the templates, to ensure that there are no gaps left between them. Pin, then tack these shapes in place, using the sewn design lines for positioning; start with templates H and D. Use a herringbone stitch to attach each piece along all of its edges.

5 Continue to sew down petals A, B, C, E and F and work a turned edge on each of these pieces (see pages 50–51), using an invisible slip stitch and a coordinating machine thread. Create some ruching and texture as you sew.

6 Fray some sheer black fabrics, in both directions, for interest. Cut templates G, I and J from these, and apply with a small coordinating stab stitch (not shown).

7 Back several small pieces of velvet with iron-on interfacing to stabilise their edges. Use appliqué stitch to secure them on top of some areas of the sheer fabrics (refer to the template and finished item for guidance).

8 To create the stamens, take your piece of black organdy fabric, and fray one long edge. Sew a running stitch along the unfrayed edge and gather it up into a ruffle. Pin the gathered shape in the centre of your poppy, as per the template, then use appliqué stitch to secure it.

9 Add some bullion knots with embroidery stranded cotton, and pistil stitches (see pages 123 and 122) using a fine machine thread, around the lower edges of the fabric ruffle. Also add some beads on top of and behind the frayed ruffle.

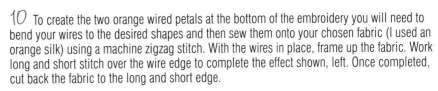

10 To create the two orange wired petals at the bottom of the embroidery you will need to bend your wires to the desired shapes and then sew them onto your chosen fabric (I used an orange silk) using a machine zigzag stitch. With the wires in place, frame up the fabric. Work long and short stitch over the wire edge to complete the effect shown, left. Once completed, cut back the fabric to the long and short edge.

11 Attach the wired petals with small stab stitches under the long and short stitch so the stitches are hidden; plunge the wires to the reverse of the frame to conceal them (not shown).

12 Now tighten the frame so that it is drum-tight, ready for the application of the carpet felt centre (not shown).

13 You will need to build up a domed centre of carpet felt in the centre of your poppy. Cut the first piece to size (with about a 5cm/2in diameter), and secure it in place using a herringbone stitch and embroidery silk. Continue to add a further two smaller circular layers on top, to create the raised shape (see also pages 43 and 45).

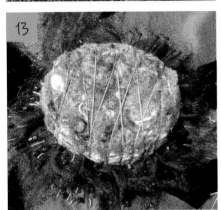

14 Layer together your variety of green silk fabrics, with the lightest on top and the darkest at the bottom. Tack all the layers together. Mark the design on the top layer of fabric using tailors' chalk so that no design lines will show once the piece has been machined. The tailors' chalk I used is a fine-line pencil used most commonly by quilters. Machine stitch your design in place using a straight stitch and a coordinating thread colour.

15 Gradually cut away layers of the fabric to reveal darker shades of silk underneath (see pages 95 and 101–102 for more detail).

16 When you are happy with the layers that are showing, work a whipped wheel onto the silk (see page 125), with some bullion knots radiating out from this. Apply small sections of satin stitch sitting around each knot.

17 Cut out your stitched circular piece, leaving a 1.5cm (½in) seam allowance. Cut notches into the seam allowance, so that the edges will turn under neatly. Diagonally tack this down on top of your carpet felt, then slip stitch around the shape to form a turned edge.

18 To complete the piece, add further bullion knots, straight stitches and beads (see pages 101–102 for more detail).

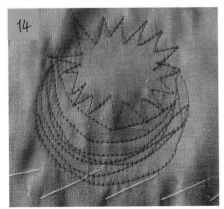

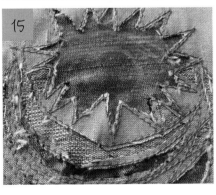

IN DETAIL

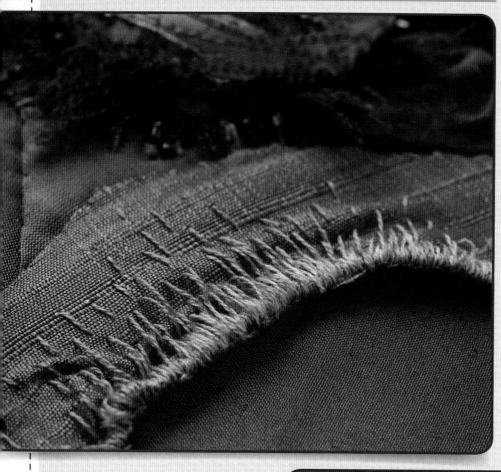

The wired petals were created by working a wide machine zigzag stitch over wire. Then a free long and short stitch was worked over the edge of the wire in a solid stitch. Subsequent rows of long and short stitch were made more open to give a sense of the petal emerging from the middle of the flower. Once all the long and short stitch has been worked, the silk dupion fabric was trimmed back to the raw edge of the long and short edge.

The frayed silk organdy was stitched down with small invisible stitches on the surface. The silk velvet was stabilised on the reverse with iron-on interfacing to prevent fraying and then appliqué stitched around the edge of the piece.

Layers of fabric were cut back as a reverse appliqué technique so that the centre of the poppy looked organic and naturalistic. The poppy's head was finished with a gathered piece of black frayed organdy underneath the head and then the slip was stitched down over carpet felt with a turned edge.

This image shows the layering up of fabric, which I achieved mostly through tacking and using paper templates. No painting of design lines was done for this project. The background petals are stitched with loose stem and running stitch in one strand of embroidery cotton. To give a sense of depth to the black marks on the petal, I frayed a piece of black organdy and appliqué stitched a stabilised piece of silk velvet over the top.

Once the slip had been applied to the frame over the top of the frayed organdy, pistil stitch and beads were added to look like stamens; bullion knots also created a matt effect.

To complete the centre of the poppy I used a whipped wheel stitch that was surrounded in bullion knots and satin stitch blocks. These were worked on the slip prior to application to the carpet felt.

APPLIQUÉ INSPIRATION

Early Morning
30 x 24cm (12 x 9½in)
Elaine Dunn

The piece is based on a sepia pen and brush picture by Samuel Palmer,
dated 1825. It gave lots of opportunity for padding and layering, and for fabric
surface embroidery.

Cockcrow (original stained glass, right)

Helen Robinson, www.orielglassstudio.co.uk

Stained glass and textiles share many commonalities: manipulation of luminous colour, layered translucency and often graphic pattern design all bound together by skilled craftsmanship. Cockcrow was originally made for an exhibition of panels by members of the British Society of Master Glass Painters in 2004. It demonstrates intricate techniques: acid etching of 'flashed' glass, several layers plated together, then painted, stained and kiln-fired before being assembled with lead – skills ancient and modern and a jubilant reversal of the concept that traditional stained glass is a lost art.

Rooster in Stitch (embroidered work, below)

43 x 43cm (17 x 17in)

Teresa McAuliffe

This piece was directly inspired by Helen Robinson's stained glass original. The possibilities of different fabrics were explored here: the shiny side of a piece of red leather was used for the tongue while the matt side was used for the cockerel's head. The pattern on the batik material on the 'waistcoat' and the tail feathers was embroidered with threads, beads and sequins. The defining moment was finding some tiny bells for the ends of the cockerel's neck and leg feathers, which are reminiscent of a jester's costume.

104

The Full English
36 x 52cm (14 x 20½in)
Annalee Levin

This piece is an attempt to immortalise the famous English breakfast in a fun and whimsical manner. It incorporates such elements as individually padded beans, stuffed tomatoes, and toast made of quilt wadding (batting) covered in a marmalade of shimmery fabric and bullion knots.

Along the Missouri
42 x 27cm (16½ x 10½in)
Sara-Jane Dennis

This piece is taken from an image by George Barbier, 1922. It is worked on habotai silk using various fabrics and threads.

Moonlight
17 x 37cm (6²/₃ x 14²/₃in)
Alana Chenevix-Trench

This piece is inspired by the artist Alphonse Mucha. The figure's dress has been made with various thicknesses of felt, carpet felt, wadding (batting) and padding, covered by different shades of blue silk. The moon shows machine embroidery and couched pearl-purl at the edges. Lots of beads, sequins and shisha mirrors were used for the background, and twenty-six wired petals with buttonhole stitch for the headdress.

Pied Piper

91 x 55cm (36 x 21¾in)

M. Helsdon, courtesy of the Embroiderers' Guild

A panel in machine appliqué using furnishing fabrics; made in Britain in 1960.

USING SHEER FABRIC FOR APPLIQUÉ

Shadow-work, or chikan embroidery, originates in India. It is a beautiful technique worked with sheer fabrics, and the results remind me of stained glass. It is usually considered to be a whitework technique but there are elements of appliqué within it and it has a lot of potential for appliqué layers. Shadow-work appliqué allows you to layer and create different depths of sheers with stitches that show through from the reverse of the frame. For this technique it is best to use a substantial cotton sheer fabric – my preference is cotton organdy as it has substance and is not slippery; it also dyes very well. To transfer your design, trace it off onto the organdy with an HB propelling pencil for a fine line or if you find this hard to see, use a water-erasable fabric pen.

When working shadow-work, all the appliqué elements should be applied first and then closed herringbone stitch and any other decorative stitches are worked. I will be showing you how to apply fabric and how to work the closed herringbone stitch.

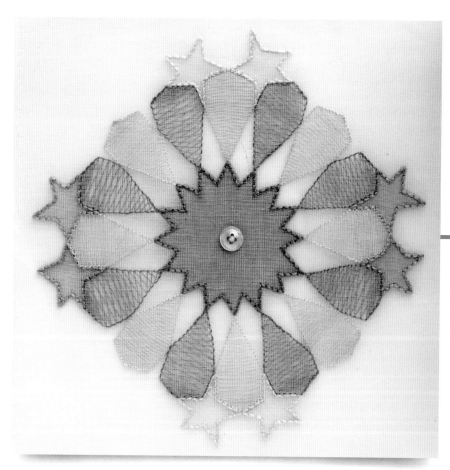

Islamic Tile Motif
12 x 12cm (4¾ x 4¾in)
Kate Cross

Shadow-work sampler containing appliqué worked with pin stitch and closed herringbone stitch.

SHADOW-WORK

This stitch is traditionally worked in shadow-work for applying fabrics.
The fabric for applying is initially pinned and then tacked onto the reverse
of the frame using a diagonal tacking stitch so that both fabrics are at similar
tensions. Once the fabric is tacked you can then place your work into a ring
frame. Pin stitch appliqué is worked in wider areas of the design where closed
herringbone would become too loose over a wide area.

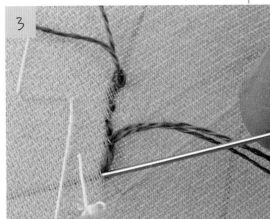

PIN STITCH

I have chosen to work with two strands of embroidery cotton but you could choose to work
with one for a more delicate effect.

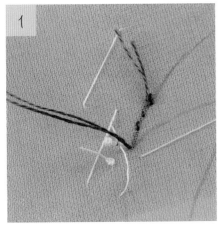

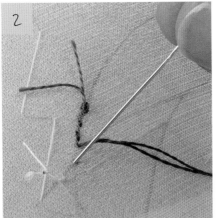

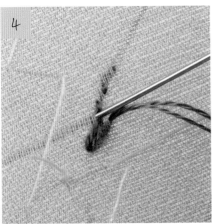

1 Thread up a size 9 embroidery needle, or similar, with two strands of embroidery
thread. Knot the tail and cast on with two stitches. Bring up the needle through the
fabric's surface at the base of the cast-on stitches.

2 Take the needle back down to the point of the shape.

3 Work a backstitch over this initial stitch to create a double layer of threads.

4 Trim away the knot. Come up diagonally opposite where you took your needle
down last so that you are making a small stitch into the fabric and take your needle
back down into the first hole you made with your stitch.

5 Continue to work pairs of identical backstitches on top of one another, and then a
smaller pin stitch that bites into both fabrics. If you are working this stitch correctly,
it should resemble a buttonhole stitch on the surface.

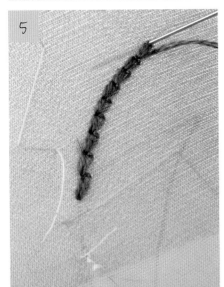

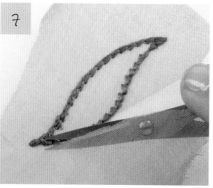

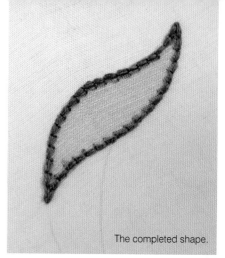

The completed shape.

6 Work all the way around the shape until you get back to the start. Cast off the threads by running them through previous stitches on the reverse. Cut your diagonal tacking stitches and remove them.

7 Take your embroidery out of the frame and turn the work over to the reverse so you can see the applied fabric. Cut away the top layer of sheer fabric, right up to the pin stitch edge, using either curved scissors or appliqué scissors to prevent you snipping through the sheer front.

Getting a close cut

When cutting the appliqué on the reverse it is sometimes easier to cut around the pin stitch leaving some excess fabric the first time, and then cut right up to the pin stitch the second time round for a crisp edge.

CLOSED HERRINGBONE STITCH

This stitch operates on the reverse of the fabric. It is best worked with a fine thread in a small embroiderer's needle. When casting on and casting off stitches, make sure you make them small so that they can be easily concealed.

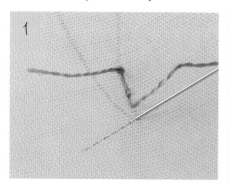

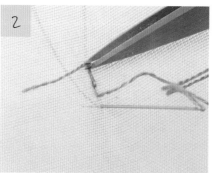

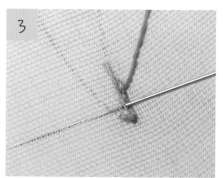

1 Thread up your needle, knot the thread tail and then cast on with two stitches, close to the bottom of your design. Bring up the needle through the fabric's surface at the base of your cast-on stitches.

2 Cut away the knot. Take a small stitch roughly 3mm (¹/₈in) long back down to the tip of the shape.

3 Come up on the left-hand side of the shape, 3mm (¹/₈in) away from the tip of the shape and make a stitch back to the point of the shape. Then come up on the right-hand side, again 3mm (¹/₈in) away from the first stitch, and take the needle back down into the hole.

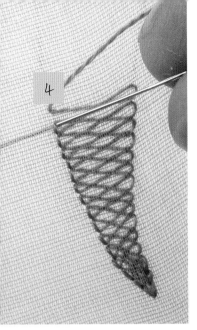

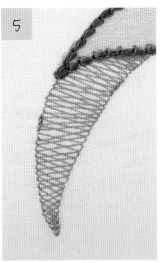

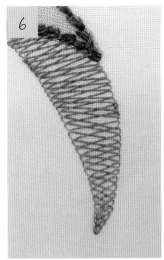

4 Continue to work stitches alternately on the left- and right-hand sides of the design so that you form a herringbone stitch on the back and a small backstitch on the front that covers the design lines.

5 Work the stitch right up to the top of the shape.

6 This is what the piece looks like from the back.

Working irregular shapes

When working a shape where one side is longer than the other, as in the tail of this paradise bird, elongate your backstitches a fraction on the longer design line, as this will keep the herringbone stitch operating at a similar angle across the shape, rather than diagonally.

Paradise Bird

18 x 11cm (7 x 4½in)

Kate Cross

This piece is worked using space-dyed cotton threads and metallics. The techniques include herringbone stitch, shadow-work appliqué, fishbone stitch, running stitch and pulled work.

Covering large areas

Herringbone stitch has limitations as to widths of area that it can be worked across, as it tends to sag on the reverse over larger areas. When working a larger area, why not split the areas up into sections as I have done in the bird's tail?

EMBROIDERY STITCHES

When I design an appliqué piece I form a plan that works as a guide to which stitches are appropriate for different areas. I have a key set of stitches that I turn to for different uses, and I have included some of them for you to refer to. To cover edges that have been sewn down with appliqué stitch you can use decorative stitches such as couching, stem stitch, chain, blanket, fishbone and satin stitch. I have also included a few other stitches that I have used in some of my projects, as they are appropriate for very fine, detailed areas where appliqué might not be as successful.

All the stitches are demonstrated using two strands of stranded embroidery thread, but you can use more or fewer threads depending on the density of stitch desired; also experiment with other threads such as perlé, silk or wool for different exciting effects.

Casting off

To cast off threads, either do so with two small stitches on the front of the fabric on an area you are going to cover with subsequent stitching, or on a design line. If there are no available design lines to work on within 1cm (½in) of the stitch then turn your frame over and cast the thread off on the reverse by running your needle back and forth for 2.5cm (1in) through previous stitching and then cut off any excess thread.

RUNNING STITCH

This is a simple stitch that can be worked on its own or in a block. Generally, running stitch is worked with evenly sized stitches and evenly sized gaps. However, the lengths of the stitch can be altered to create a shaded effect, as I have demonstrated in the Poppy project (see pages 94–102).

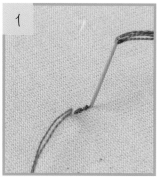
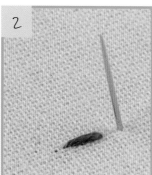

1 Thread up a size 9 embroidery needle, or similar, with two strands of embroidery thread. Knot the tail and then cast on with two stitches, then cut off the knot so you are ready to begin the stitch.

2 Come up with the needle at the start of the two casting on stitches and take the needle down over the top of the casting on stitches so that the initial stitches are covered.

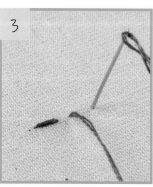

3 Bring up the needle in front of the first stitch and then take the needle down again to create a stitch the same size.

4 Continue to repeat this until a line of running stitch is complete.

BACKSTITCH

This is one of the most basic stitches that can be used for fine details in embroidery. Usually backstitch is worked so that each stitch is the same size, but stitches can be enlarged or reduced for effect.

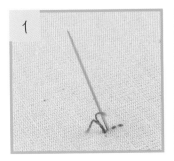

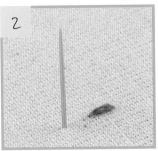

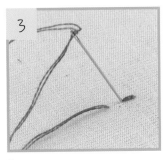

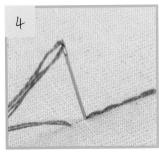

1 Thread up a size 9 embroidery needle, or similar, with two strands of embroidery thread. Knot the tail and then cast on with two stitches. Cut off the knot so you are ready to begin the stitch.

2 Bring up the needle at the left of the two casting on stitches and take it down to the right, over the top of the casting on stitches to cover them.

3 Bring up the needle to the left of the first stitch. Take it down to the right, into the hole at the left-hand side of the first stitch to create an identical second stitch.

4 Continue working in the same way to create a line of backstitch.

COUCHING

Couching is a method of attaching a single thread or a selection of threads using a separate thread, which is stitched over the core couching threads at regular intervals. This technique is usually used to neaten off and conceal initial appliqué stitches that secure pieces of fabric down, but it can also be worked as a stitch in its own right for finer details in appliqué. If you are using this as an appliqué edge technique, take a look at the size of the appliqué stitch you are concealing when deciding how many threads to use for your core thread, and this will guide you. Always strand out your threads and place them back together so they are not twisted (see page 60).

1 Thread up a size 9 embroidery needle, or similar, with two strands of embroidery thread. Knot the tail and then cast on with two stitches. Cut off the knot. Bring up the needle at the start of the two casting on stitches and take the needle down over the top of the core couching threads so that the initial stitches are covered by the core threads.

2 Continue making stitches at regular intervals to secure the core threads to the fabric surface.

3 Work a series of stitches. Once complete, the couching thread should be cast off on the reverse and the core threads can be plunged through to the reverse of the frame and secured with a curved needle and a double length of machine thread.

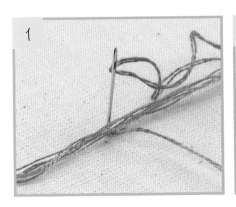

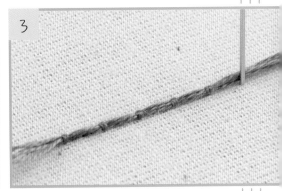

STEM STITCH

This stitch is especially useful for getting around corners and working small areas and can be used for outlining and working small curved areas with accuracy; I commonly use it for fine text. It is worked so that each stitch is even in size. The stitch is worked from bottom to top of a shape and the loop is always held to the right-hand side of the needle. Stitches are not pulled tightly and are worked at a loose tension so that the stitch sits on the fabric surface and resembles a rope. If you accidently hold the loop to the left-hand side then it creates a differing twist and is known as outline stitch.

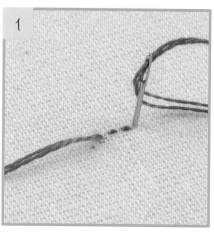

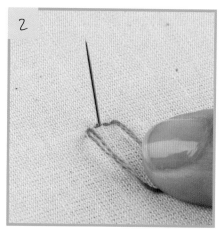

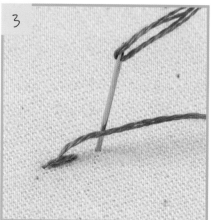

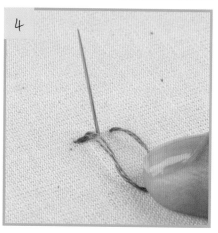

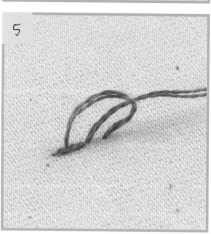

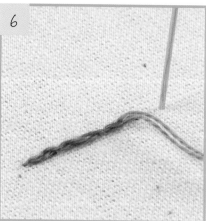

1 Thread up a size 9 embroidery needle, or similar, with two strands of embroidery thread. Knot the tail, cast on with two stitches, then cut off the knot so you are ready to begin the stitch. Bring up the needle at the start of the two casting on stitches and take the needle down to the left, over the top of the casting on stitches so that they are covered.

2 Before you pull the stitch tight on the fabric's surface, bring up the needle in the middle of the first stitch, holding the first stitch to the right-hand side. Pull the needle through at the mid-point of the first stitch and pull the stitch so that it sits on the fabric surface.

3 Take the needle down in front of the first stitch so that this second stitch is the same size as the first. Again, do not pull the stitch tight.

4 Hold the loop of thread to the right-hand side and bring up the needle in the mid-point of the stitch.

5 Pull the thread through so that the stitch sits flat on the surface.

6 Continuously work this stitch to create a rope-like effect.

CHAIN STITCH

Chain stitch is a decorative stitch that is formed from a series of interlocking loops and can be used for outlining. The loops should be identically sized with a relatively loose tension.

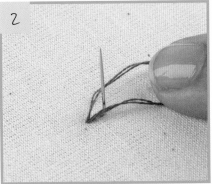
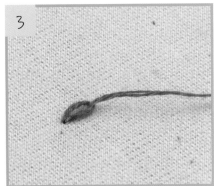
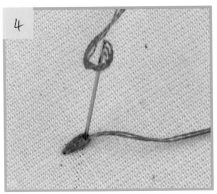
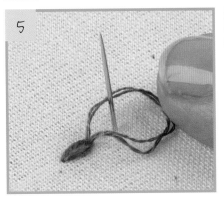
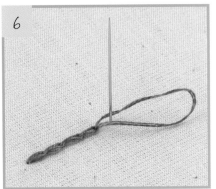

1 Thread up a size 9 embroidery needle, or similar, with two strands of embroidery thread. Knot the tail, cast on with two stitches, then cut off the knot so you are ready to begin the stitch. Bring up the needle at the start of the two casting on stitches and take the needle back down into the same hole to create a loop on the fabric's surface.

2 Bring up your needle to the right, within the loop of thread.

3 Pull the needle through onto the surface of the fabric and as you do so the tension of the loop should increase to create a flat loop.

4 Take the needle back down into the same hole you came up at in step 3 and create another loop on the fabric's surface.

5 Bring up your needle to the right, within the loop of thread.

6 Continue to work this stitch until required.

7 To complete the stitch, bring up your needle in the last loop and make a small stitch over the end of the last loop of the chain stitch.

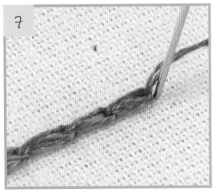

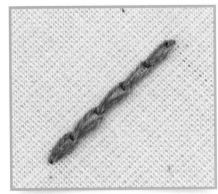

Completed length of chain stitch.

BUTTONHOLE STITCH

Buttonhole stitch, also known as blanket stitch, can be used for covering a raw edge of applied fabric. There are many variations of buttonhole and it is used as a base to needlelace in stumpwork embroidery.

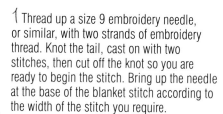

1 Thread up a size 9 embroidery needle, or similar, with two strands of embroidery thread. Knot the tail, cast on with two stitches, then cut off the knot so you are ready to begin the stitch. Bring up the needle at the base of the blanket stitch according to the width of the stitch you require.

2 Take your needle back down next to where you came up – this distance will determine the spacing between each stitch. Don't pull the thread tight – leave a loop.

3 Come up at the point of your two cast on stitches, directly opposite your initial stitch, and catch the loop with your needle.

4 Pull the needle through to tighten the loop. Take the needle down at the base of the stitch, using the same spacing to form another loop on the fabric's surface.

5 Bring up the needle in line with your cast-on stitches; catch the loop at the top of the stitch.

6 Take the needle down into the fabric at the base of the stitch to form another loop.

7 Catch the loop at the top of the stitch to complete the row of buttonhole stitches.

8 Take the needle down outside, but close to, the loop of thread to secure the stitch.

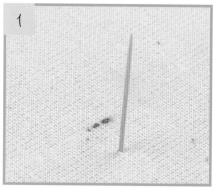

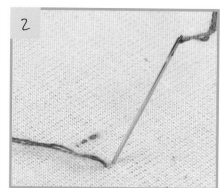

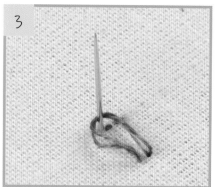

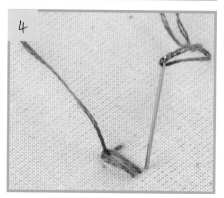

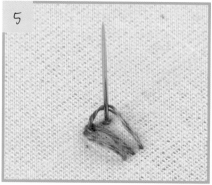

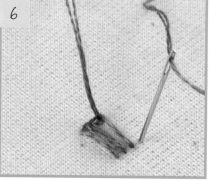

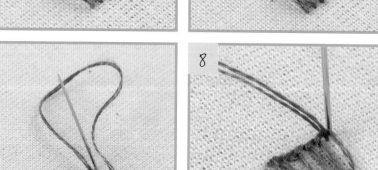

The completed stitch.

SPLIT STITCH

This stitch is often used as a base for other stitches, as it helps to stabilise the edges of solid stitches such as satin stitch, raised satin and long and short stitch. It is also useful for outlining very small shapes where stem stitch is too large – it forms a stitch that resembles miniature chain stitch.

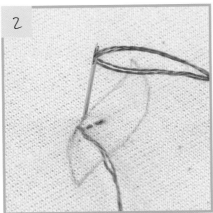
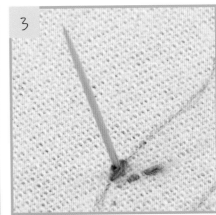

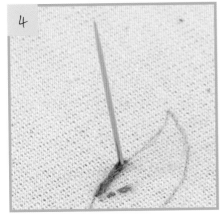
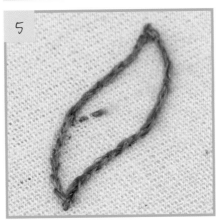
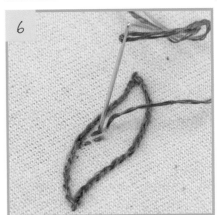

1 Thread up a size 9 embroidery needle, or similar, with two strands of embroidery thread. Knot the tail, cast on with two stitches, then cut off the knot so you are ready to begin the stitch. Bring up the needle on the design line you are working.

2 Take the needle down in front on the line to create a stitch that is around 2mm (1/16in) long.

3 Bring your needle back up through the middle of this initial stitch.

4 Continue to take your needle down ahead of the stitch and then come back up from underneath to split each stitch in half.

5 Work this all the way around the shape.

6 Cast off in the shape that you are filling with two casting off stitches, or finish off on a design line, or on the reverse of the stitching if there are no available design lines to work on.

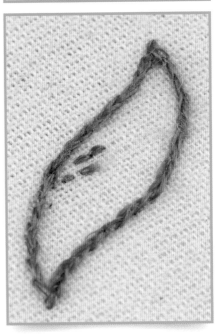

The completed stitch.

FISHBONE STITCH

This stitch is usually worked in a leaf-shaped area by alternating diagonal stitches – this creates a central vein down the middle of the shape. When working this stitch it is useful to put this middle line onto the shape for a guide as to where to take down your needle. Fishbone stitch is always worked from the narrowest shape to the widest.

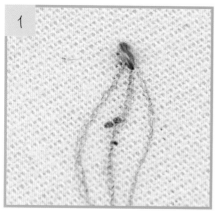

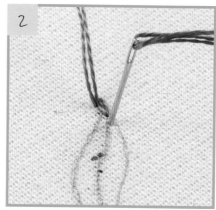

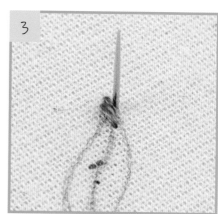

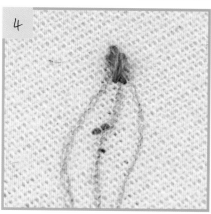

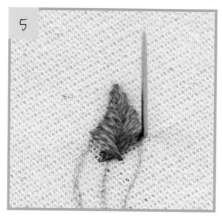

The completed stitch.

1 Thread up a size 9 embroidery needle, or similar, with two strands of embroidery thread. Knot the tail, cast on with two stitches, then cut off the knot so you are ready to begin the stitch. Create a small stitch at the tip of the shape; work from the top of the shape down onto the central line.

2 Bring up the needle next to the first stitch on the outer edge of the shape. Bring the needle down to create a diagonal stitch that finishes on the central line.

3 Bring up the needle, this time on the right-hand side of the top stitch.

4 Bring the needle down to create a diagonal stitch that sits slightly to the left of the central line and overlaps the stitch made in step 2.

5 Continue bringing up your needle on the outside design line alternating from the left to the right with each stitch. You will start to create a solid area of fishbone stitch.

Why not try...
Fishbone can also be worked over split stitch to stabilise edges and create a raised area of embroidered work.

SATIN STITCH

This is a solid stitch that is used to fill in areas and create relief and lustrous texture. This stitch works well over small areas but loses its tension when worked larger than 1cm (½in). Satin stitch can also be padded underneath to form padded satin stitch (see pages 120–121).

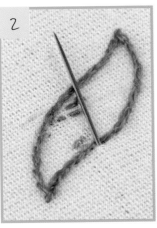

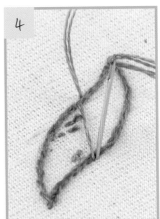

The completed stitch.

1 Thread up a size 9 embroidery needle, or similar, with two strands of embroidery thread. Knot the tail, cast on with two stitches, then cut off the knot so you are ready to begin the stitch.

2 Bring up the needle outside the split stitch outline at the middle of the shape you are working. You will be working the top half of the shape first, then returning to complete the bottom.

3 Take your needle down on the opposite side of the split stitch shape to create a 45-degree angle. Bring up your needle at the wider angle and take it down at the smaller angle to create a consistently angled stitch.

4 Bring the needle back up next to the point you took it down. Bring the thread back over the top of the shape and insert the needle next to your initial stitch to ensure that the threads lie close to each other. You will be bringing up and taking down the needle on the same side to avoid long stitches on the reverse of the fabric.

5 Continue working the stitch, coming up at the wider angle of the stitch and taking your needle down at the smaller, making sure all of these stitches sit outside the split stitch outline.

6 Work the final stitch at the very tip of the shape.

7 Return to the middle of the shape and work satin stitch back down to the bottom of the shape. Again, you should be bringing your needle up at the wider angle and taking your needle down at the smaller angle. Complete with a small stitch at the base.

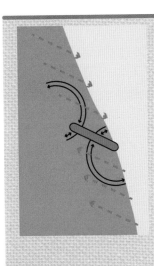

Working at an angle

Once you have set your angle with your first stitch you should always come up with your needle at the wider angle and take your needle down at the smaller angle.

USING PADDED SATIN STITCH

Padded satin stitch is traditionally used in whitework embroidery but is very useful when working small dimensional areas of your embroidery where string padding is too bulky. It is built up using alternating layers of padding within the outer edge of the stitch. I would advise not working this stitch over an area any larger than 1cm (½in) as it loses its tension.

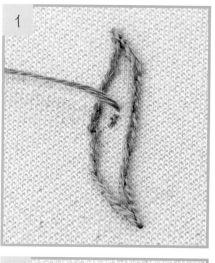

1 Work a small split stitch around the outer edge of the design area.

2 Work an initial area of diagonal stitches from the middle to the top, making long stitches in the centre of the area. Bring up and take down the needle on the same side to avoid long stitches on the reverse of the fabric.

3 Work from the middle to the bottom of the shape with your first layer of padding in the same way.

4 Work the second layer of padding in the opposite diagonal direction, so that the stitches sit on top of the first set and do not slip down into the first layer of padding. Again, work from the middle to the tip of the shape and then return to the middle to work the other half of the shape to keep the angle of the padding stitches.

5 The second row of padding is complete.

6 The third and final row of padding sits again at an alternate diagonal angle to the last and sits right up to the inside of the split stitch. Start the padding in the middle of the shape and work one half of the shape.

7 Return to the middle of the shape and work from the middle to the bottom to complete the third layer of padding.

8 The third row of padding is complete.

9 Work the final layer on the outside edge of the split stitch. Create your first stitch in the opposite diagonal direction to your third layer of padding. Then for your second stitch come up at the wider angle on your shape that has been set with your initial stitch.

10 Continue to work up to the top of the shape, always coming up with your needle at the widest angle and taking your needle down at the smaller angle on the shape. In doing so you are wrapping around the shape and creating a large stitch on the reverse of the fabric.

11 Once you have completed one half of the shape return to the middle and come up with your needle at the wider angle and down at the smaller to wrap the shape in stitch.

12 Once you reach the bottom point, cast off the thread in an area of design near to the stitch that will be covered in subsequent fabric or stitch or, alternatively, turn the frame over and gently pass the needle under the wrapped stitches. Cut off the remaining thread.

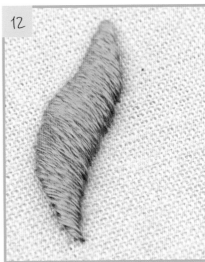

FRENCH KNOT

French knots can be worked singly or in clusters. They are made larger by adding further threads in the needle rather than wrapping more times around the needle. When working French knots for the first time, try using one thread, as you will have more control over one thread than many.

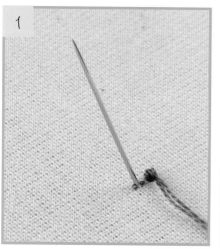

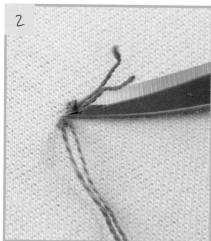

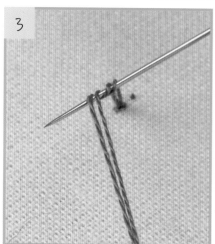

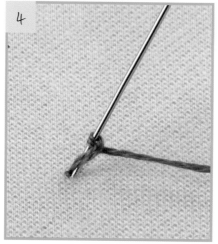

1 Thread up a size 9 embroidery needle, or similar, with two strands of embroidery thread. Knot the tail and cast on with two stitches. Bring up your needle next to the casting on stitches.

2 Cut off the casting on knot – snip as close to the fabric as you can.

3 Take the thread around the needle once to form one entire wrap.

4 Take the needle down next to where you came up to cover the two initial cast on stitches. Ensure that you are not taking the needle down in the same hole, or the knot will disappear to the reverse of the fabric. Hold the thread tight to keep a firm tension.

5 Push the needle down through the loop whilst holding the thread to keep it tensioned.

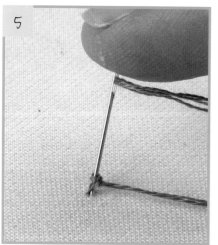

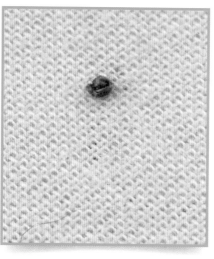

Filling with French knots

To fill an area with French knots, come up at a French knot's size distance away from the original knot – take the needle back towards the first knot as you make the stitch. Continue to work knots back to the previous one to fill an area entirely.

Making pistil stitch

To modify this stitch and create a pistil stitch, take the knot back down into the fabric a short distance from where you initially brought it up, to create a 'tail'.

A completed French knot.

BULLION KNOT

Bullion knots are larger, longer versions of French knots and can be worked alone or in clusters. I find they are really useful for creating details such as stamens in flowers and birds' claws.

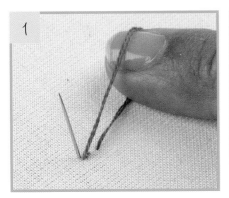
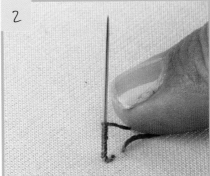
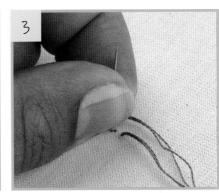

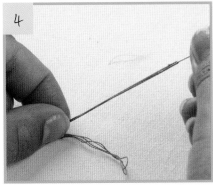
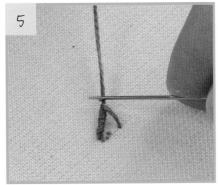
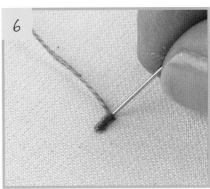

A completed bullion knot.

1 Thread up a size 9 embroidery needle, or similar, with two strands of embroidery thread. Knot the tail, cast on with two stitches, then cut off the knot so you are ready to begin the stitch. Bring up the needle at the start of the two casting on stitches and take the needle down over the casting on stitches to create a loop on the fabric's surface. The size of this first stitch will determine the length of the knot. Bring up the needle partway through the fabric, at the start of the first stitch.

2 Take the loop and wrap this around the needle. Do so by rotating the needle from underneath. Create enough wraps on the needle to fill the stitch length, but don't overwrap it – if you work too many loops on the needle the stitch will sit proud on the fabric surface.

3 Hold the loops loosely on the needle with your fingers.

4 Pull the needle up through the loops, supporting the loops with your other hand.

5 Push the loops down evenly using your needle.

6 Take the needle back down into the fabric next to where you began your stitch and took your needle down in step 1.

Make bullion knots easy

If you find bullion knots tricky, practise French knots first. It is also worth trying to use one thread rather than two or more, as you will have more control over one single thread. A larger, finer needle can also help – if you are struggling with an embroidery needle, try using a straw needle.

WOVEN WHEEL

These are worked using an odd number of spokes and as the size increases you should use more spokes. They make fantastic centres to flowers.

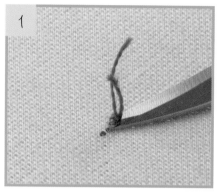
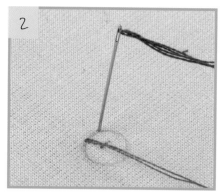

1 Thread up a size 9 embroidery needle or similar size with two strands of embroidery thread, knot the tail and then cast on with two stitches, then cut off the knot so you are ready to begin the stitch.

2 Create a fly stitch by coming up on the outside edge of the circle and then taking the needle down on the opposite edge to create a loop on the fabric surface. You are dividing the circle into one fifth in this instance.

3 Catch the loop in the centre of the circle.

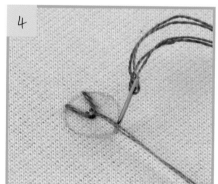

4 Take the needle down on the opposite side of the circle to form a third spoke.

5 Bring up your needle on the lower right-hand side and create a stitch that goes back in towards the middle of the circle.

6 Make a final spoke from the left-hand side to the centre. The shape is divided evenly into five sections.

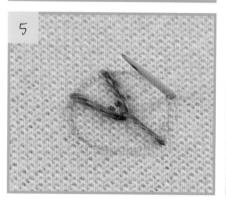
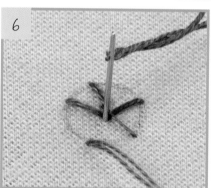

7 Change your thread, if you want to add a new colour, and cast on. Bring up your needle between the spokes at the central point.

8 Change to a tapestry needle and weave up and under each spoke to form a basket weave from the centre out.

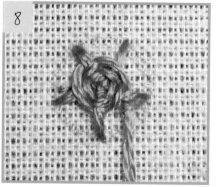

The completed stitch.

REFERENCE

124

WHIPPED WHEEL

This stitch is similar to the woven wheel but it gives more of a textured centre and can be worked over an even or an odd number of spokes.

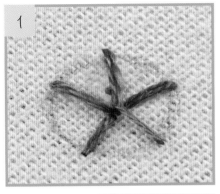

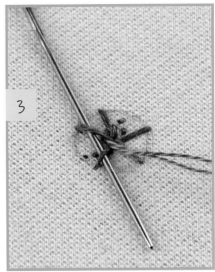

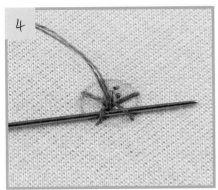

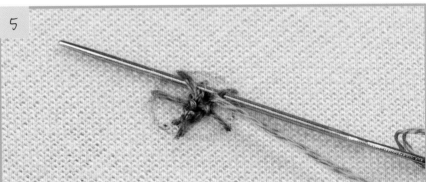

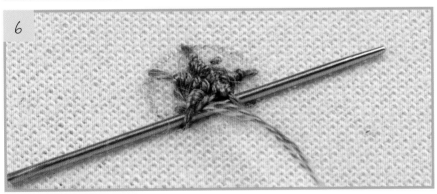

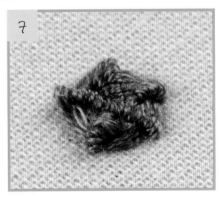

1 Create the spokes by creating an initial fly stitch and then by subsequently adding further spokes so that the circle is divided evenly (see steps 1–8, page 124).

2 Cast on at the middle of the wheel with another thread, or use the same one that you used for the spokes. Then change your needle to a blunt-ended tapestry needle and create a wrap on the first spoke and take the needle under the next spoke.

3 Create another wrap or loop on the next spoke and slide your needle under the following spoke.

4 Continue to wrap the third spoke with one loop of thread.

5 Return back to where you started so that all the spokes have one wrap of thread on them at the centre of the circle.

6 Continue this sequence around the spokes until they are completely covered.

7 Secure your thread with two hidden stitches tucked under the wheel on a design line, or cast off on the reverse.

NEEDLES

This needle information is reproduced with permission from John James needle specialists, www.jjneedles.com.

SHARPS

These are general-purpose sewing needles used by dressmakers. Size 16, 17 and 18 are known as Carpet Sharps and, as their name suggests, are most commonly used in the design and manufacture of carpets and rugs.

TAPESTRY OR CROSS-STITCH

These large-eyed needles allow the user to thread tapestry wool or six-stranded cotton easily. The blunt tapestry point enables the needle to pass through canvas without tearing or splitting its fibres. Available in sizes 13–28.

LEATHER OR GLOVERS'

These needles have unusual triangulated (cutting) points to enable them to pass through tough materials without causing unnecessary abrasion. While, as their name suggests, they were originally intended for use when leather working, they are also ideal when working with other media such as suede and soft plastics.

DARNERS

Long and sharp with elongated eyes, as their name suggests, these are used for darning or mending. Sizes 14 to 18 are commonly known as Yarn or Wool Darners.

CHENILLE

These are identical to Tapestry or Cross-stitch needles in length and diameter but the Chenille point is sharp, enabling the needle to pass through the coarsest of fabrics.

CURVED

Curved needles are measured in length around the bend as well as by gauge (the thickness of the needles). The higher the gauge the finer the needle. Curved needles are extremely useful across a variety of craft work and in the upholstery trades.

EMBROIDERY OR CREWEL

Embroidery needles have a longer eye than a standard Sharps needle, making them more suitable for threading stranded cotton. Apart from this, their length, diameter and point profile is akin to that of a Sharps needle.

MILLINERS' OR STRAWS

Although traditionally used in the Millinery trade, these needles are now more commonly used for pleating, fancy decorative stitching or even some types of beadwork. They are similar to an ordinary Sharps needle but longer.

LONG DARNERS

Another form of darning needle, the extra length and larger eyes make these even more suitable for mending with wool or other thick and coarse threads.

QUILTING OR BETWEENS

Specifically designed for quilters, the short length of these needles allows you to stitch far more quickly than when using an ordinary sewing needle.

EASY THREADING OR CALYX EYE

Ideal for those who find it difficult to thread regular needles, these are standard needles with a cut made in the top of the eye to allow thread to pass through it from above.

BEADING

Beading needles are made from the finest steel wire, enabling their use with beads, sequins and pearls. Short beading or Bead embroidery needles are specially created Beading needles whose diameters match those of the regular Beading needles, yet in very short lengths. They are ideal for embellishing garments with both beads or sequins and sections of hand embroidery. As with the Short beading needles, the diameters of Tapestry pointed short beading and Ball point bead embroidery needles match those of regular Beading needles, yet in very short lengths. As an additional feature, these needles have a specially rounded Tapestry-style point enabling the user to embellish pieces of cross-stitch or tapestry with beads, sequins or pearls without splitting the fibres of the canvas.

SUPPLIERS

The Royal School of Needlework online shop:

www.royal-needlework.org.uk/shop

UK-based suppliers:

Barnett Lawson Trimmings: www.bltrimmings.com

Cloth House: www.clothhouse.com

DMC: www.dmc.com

For cord winders: www.annacrutchley.co.uk

For felt: www.weircrafts.com/wool-felt/wool-felt.html

For silk: www.thesilkroute.co.uk

Golden Threads: www.goldenthreads.co.uk

MacCulloch & Wallis Ltd: www.macculloch-wallis.co.uk

Needles by John James: www.jjneedles.com

Out of Africa: www.outofafricaquilts.co.uk

The Cotton Patch: www.cottonpatch.co.uk

The Crazy Wire Company: www.wireandstuff.co.uk

The Eternal Maker: www.eternalmaker.com

Toye & Co: www.thetoyeshop.com/benton-johnson.html

US-based suppliers:

Coats: www.makeitcoats.com/en-us

Connecting Threads: www.connectingthreads.com

Fat Quarter Shop: www.fatquartershop.com

Other:

Chertsey Museum: www.chertseymuseum.org

The D-Day Museum: www.ddaymuseum.co.uk

The Embroiderers' Guild: www.embroiderersguild.com

The Hastings Museum and Art Gallery: www.hmag.org.uk

The Sunbury Embroidery Gallery: www.sunburygallery.org

FURTHER READING

RSN Essential Stitch Guides: Crewelwork by Jacqui McDonald

RSN Essential Stitch Guides: Stumpwork by Kate Sinton

RSN Essential Stitch Guides: Whitework by Lizzy Lansberry

Art of Embroidery: The Royal School of Needlework – A History of Style and Design by Lanto Synge

A World of Embroidery by Mary Gostelow

Colour: The Professional's Guide by Karen Triedman

Color Theory by Patti Mollica

Contemporary Whitework by Tracy A. Franklin and Nicola Jarvis

Mola Art by Kit S. Kapp

New Ideas in Goldwork by Tracy A. Franklin

World Textiles: A Concise History by Mary Schoeser

The Absolute Beginner's Guide to Patchwork, Quilting and Appliqué by Elaine Hammond

The Art of Manipulating Fabric by Colette Wolff

The Quilter's Bible by Linda Clements

The Quilts of the British Isles by Janet Rae

5000 Years of Textiles by Jennifer Harris

GLOSSARY

Base fabric: or 'ground fabric'. This is the layer of fabric that supports all appliqué and acts as a background. This is used when fabrics that are being applied are lightweight. Often linen and calico (muslin) are framed up for this purpose.

Bumf: or 'bump'. This is a heavy cotton interlining that can be rolled up to create a pounce brush.

Calico: an inexpensive part-processed cotton that comes in three weights. The material has very little stretch so is ideal for creating a background fabric to work on. Calico is known as 'muslin' in the US.

Domette: this is an interlining that is available in the widest variety of weights and finishes and is commonly used to improve the draping of curtains. It can be used for quilting and is an alternative to bumf.

Grain: a technical term that describes the direction in which your fabric has been woven.

Lasso: a loop of buttonhole thread that you create in a needle by threading both ends of the thread through the eye of the needle in opposite directions. A lasso allows you to catch short ends of thread and plunge them to the reverse of your work and cast off.

Mellor: an embroidery tool that allows you to manipulate, lay threads down and push threads into place.

Pounce: traditionally made up of ground cuttlefish or charcoal, it is used for transferring embroidery designs onto fabric.

Pouncing: transferring a design onto fabric by rubbing pounce through a perforated or 'pricked' embroidery design.

Pricker: an embroidery tool that fits a needle into its tip and enables you to prick out designs.

Reverse appliqué: where fabrics are layered up and then cut away from the top layer of fabric to reveal differing colours and textures of fabrics underneath.

Slate frame: a frame usually made from beech wood and constructed with 'arms' and 'rollers' between which fabric is stretched to give a tight tension. Generally, they come in 45.75cm (18in) and 61cm (24in) lengths, but can be found in other sizes.

Slip: this is a cut piece of fabric, often embroidered, that is applied to the ground fabric usually with a turned edge so that stitching is not visible.

Stiletto: an embroidery tool that is sharp-ended and allows you to open up holes in the fabric for creating eyelets or so that larger threads such as cords can be plunged and taken to the reverse.

Trupunto: from the Italian for 'to quilt', this is a technique that creates a puffy, decorative effect. It requires at least two layers of fabric, the underside of which is slit and padded from behind, producing a raised surface on the fabric.

Vilene: a fusible adhesive that is ironed on to the reverse of fabrics to prevent fraying and comes in differing weights. It has a smooth, fabric look, retains shape and is easy to iron on.

128

INDEX

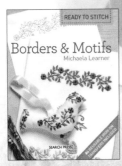
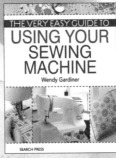
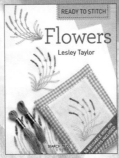

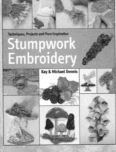

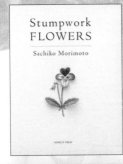

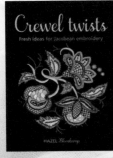
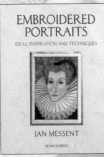
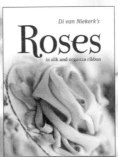

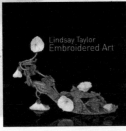
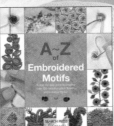
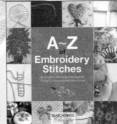